ADVOCATE

Discovering God's Heart
for Your City

ADVOCATE

Discovering God's Heart
for Your City

BRIAN HELTSLEY

ADVOCATE: Discovering God's Heart for Your City
Copyright © 2020 Brian Heltsley

All rights reserved. No part of this book may be reproduced without written permission from the publisher.

Unless otherwise indicated, all Scripture quotations are taken from the *Holy Bible*, New Living Translation, copyright © 1996, 2004, 2015 by Tyndale House Foundation. Used by permission of Tyndale House Publishers, Inc., Carol Stream, Illinois 60188. All rights reserved.

Scripture quotations marked (AMP) are taken from the Amplified® Bible, Copyright © 2015 by The Lockman Foundation. Used by permission. www.Lockman.org

Scripture quotations marked (AMPC) are taken from the Amplified® Bible, Copyright © 1954, 1958, 1962, 1964, 1965, 1987 by The Lockman Foundation. Used by permission. www.Lockman.org

Scripture quotations marked (GNT) are taken from the Good News Translation in Today's English Version-Second Edition Copyright © 1992 by American Bible Society. Used by permission.

Scripture quotations marked (NASB) are taken from the NEW AMERICAN STANDARD BIBLE®, Copyright © 1960,1962,1963,1968,1971,1972,1973,1975, 1977,1995 by The Lockman Foundation. Used by permission.

Scripture quotations marked (NIV) are taken from THE HOLY BIBLE, NEW INTERNATIONAL VERSION®, NIV® Copyright © 1973, 1978, 1984, 2011 by Biblica, Inc.® Used by permission. All rights reserved worldwide.

Printed in the United States of America

For additional information, visit
www.brianheltsley.com

Table of Contents

Chapter 1	Radical Faith for Your City	7
Chapter 2	Choosing Unconditional Love for Your City	15
Chapter 3	The Exchange of Intercession	25
Chapter 4	When Blessing Is Undeserved	39
Chapter 5	Looking at the World Through God's Eyes	57
Chapter 6	Defending Your Heart from Disappointment	69
Chapter 7	Belonging Comes Before Repentance	81
Chapter 8	Listening to Heaven First	95
Chapter 9	The Radical Agenda of God	109
Chapter 10	How Your Expectations Can Change Your City	121
Chapter 11	Becoming a True Friend of Your City	131
Chapter 12	The Good News of Rest	141
Chapter 13	From Accuser to Advocate	151
Chapter 14	Why Writing People Off Doesn't Work	165
Chapter 15	Seeing Through the Eyes of Mercy	175
Chapter 16	God's Beautiful Obsession	185
Bibliography		199

Chapter 1
RADICAL FAITH FOR YOUR CITY

When I was a drug dealer in college, I used to hitchhike from the small town of Arcata down to the big city of San Francisco to make money and attend rock concerts.

Every time I crossed the Golden Gate Bridge, I immediately began to feel a dark pressure I didn't understand. My solution to this feeling was to find the nearest liquor store, buy a forty ouncer of beer, and try to ignore the depressing sensation inside me. I was homeless at the time, and I really hated sleeping within city limits. I disliked it so much that I would often take a bus north, just across the bridge, and squat in an abandoned house. I felt much more freedom once I'd crossed the bridge and exited the city.

Many years later as a born-again Christian, I joined a group of young revivalists who visited San Francisco monthly to minister to people on the streets.

Before we left, I spent time praying and listening to Jesus to find out what He wanted to do on this trip. As I was praying, I saw a picture of one of San Francisco's prominent buildings. A massive gorilla climbed to the top and began to shake the building violently.

I didn't understand what this vision meant, but then I felt Jesus say to my heart, "This city is touchable."

Not *untouchable*. But *touchable*.

Hope and faith for this short ministry trip swept through my heart. I knew God was going to do something to *move* what I perceived to be "unmovable" hearts.

After that experience, I never saw that city, or any other, the same way again. If San Francisco is touchable, then every city is touchable. It's vulnerable to the presence of God that brings radical transformation. That day I realized God never abandons a city.

Faith for Entire Cities

If I asked you to pray for an entire city to be transformed, would you be able to do it with faith? Or does such a prayer seem impossible to you? "Yeah right! That's expecting a little too much. We don't want to set the bar too high."

Jesus, however, clearly wanted to draw everyone to Himself as He demonstrated the incredible love of God with signs and wonders. When He preached truth and manifested God's power in a region, I believe He expected everyone to repent and turn to God.

ADVOCATE

We see this in Luke 17 when a group of lepers came to Jesus for healing. He told them what to do, and as they walked away to follow His instructions, all ten were healed. But only one returned to show gratitude.

> Jesus asked, "Didn't I heal ten men? Where are the other nine? Has no one returned to give glory to God except this foreigner?"
>
> Luke 17:17-18

Jesus counted ten men healed, and I think He envisioned all ten returning and celebrating their healing. He expected all of them to worship and surrender their lives to the One who gave them hope and a brand-new start. Have you ever wondered why He would expect all of them to come back and give glory to God? Was He setting Himself up for disappointment? Or was His thinking a key to how we can step into a faith-filled mindset?

When John the Baptist's disciples approached Him, Jesus described His ministry this way:

> The blind can see, the lame can walk, those who suffer from dreaded skin diseases are made clean, the deaf hear, the dead are brought back to life, and the Good News is preached to the poor.
>
> Matthew 11:5 (GNT)

Jesus seemed to think these incredible signs should have been enough for everyone in the city to make a decision to follow Him. When He *didn't* see cities completely changed from this raw display of God's love and power, Scripture clearly reveals His disappointment: "Then Jesus began to denounce the towns where he had done so many of his miracles, because they hadn't repented of their sins and turned to God" (Matt. 11:20).

He spent a lot of time in three cities in particular—Korazin, Bethsaida, and Capernaum—and performed numerous miracles there, yet the people barely responded to Him. Deeply moved, Jesus said:

> What sorrow awaits you, Korazin and Bethsaida! For if the miracles I did in you had been done in wicked Tyre and Sidon, their people would have repented of their sins long ago, clothing themselves in burlap and throwing ashes on their heads to show their remorse.
>
> Matthew 11:21

If Jesus expected to see entire cities transformed, so should we. He gave us an example for what we should believe and have faith for—to see citywide revival.

When it comes to praying for our cities and seeing them change, our thinking needs to shift from small to *big*. Positive expectation and hope are major components in the heart of a revivalist.

"The time promised by God has come at last!" Jesus announced in Mark 1:15. "The Kingdom of God is near!"

ADVOCATE

God is present and available for anyone all the time. We need to daily remind ourselves of this truth so we can live in radical hope for our cities, the way Jesus did.

Our experiences shouldn't control how we feel about a city. Personally, I didn't like being in San Francisco. I've had some bad experiences there, but I can't allow offense to cloud my heart when I pray for this city and the precious people who live there. I feel a powerful call from God to believe again that *anything is possible* and *every city* can be radically transformed.

What if we started to pray and believe like Jesus did? What if our perspective changed forever, and we started to pray that everyone in our city would be transformed by God's love? Would that be asking too much from God, or is such a thing possible? What if this switch in mindset were the key to revival?

Stepping into Hope

When you enter a city, are you overwhelmed with hope or weighed down with pessimism?

Imagine what Jesus thought and felt when He looked at a city. His compassion overwhelmed His logic, which we repeatedly see happen in the Gospel accounts: "Jesus saw the huge crowd as he stepped from the boat, and he had compassion on them because they were like sheep without a shepherd" (Mark 6:34).

He wasn't focused on the people who *weren't* going to listen to His message—He saw all of them with hope.

When a farmer goes out to plant his seeds, he hopes and believes most of those seeds—if not all—will sprout and produce a crop. Why would we expect anything different? I think Jesus was just like that farmer. Filled with faith, He liberally poured out the goodness of His Father and expected everyone who tasted that goodness to turn their whole lives to Him.

When I am overwhelmed with God's presence, nothing else matters to me. I just want more of heaven, and I want everyone else to experience the same joy and peace I'm experiencing. I imagine it was much the same for Jesus. He was anointed with the oil of joy more than all His companions (Ps. 45:7). The glory of heaven pumped like blood through His system and filled Him with incredible hope.

Hope is not reasonable. Hope does not look at difficult circumstances and waver from its outrageous goal. Jesus had a confident expectation that *whole cities* would choose life and freedom instead of death.

I think God is frequently shocked by our responses to His lovingkindness. He gives us His whole heart, and He has great hope that He will receive ours in return.

Praying for Your City

God knows the exact number of people living in your city. If the very hairs on your head are numbered (Matt. 10:30), the people around you are certainly numbered. It doesn't matter if you live in a city of six million or four hundred—God loves *your city* and has a plan to fill it with hope (Jer. 29:11).

ADVOCATE

Jonah needed to remember how many people lived in the city God had assigned to him. He didn't want Nineveh to make it—but God obviously did. The Lord said to him, "Nineveh has more than 120,000 people living in spiritual darkness, not to mention all the animals. Shouldn't I feel sorry for such a great city?" (Jon. 4:11.)

God knew the exact number of people, and He expected every single one to repent and turn their heart to Him. And that's what happened: "Then the people of Nineveh believed in God; and they called a fast and put on sackcloth from the greatest to the least of them" (Jon. 3:5 NASB).

Is it possible for your city to be completely transformed *in a day*? Nothing is beyond God's power. We need to shift our thinking where our cities are concerned, so we can start to believe for what God wants to see happen.

We can't be afraid to set our box aside and step out into the great unknown with God, because there is nothing He cannot do.

> Who has ever seen anything as strange as this?
> Who ever heard of such a thing?
> Has a nation ever been born in a single day?
> Has a country ever come forth in a mere moment?
> Isaiah 66:8

This atmosphere of faith is the environment in which the first church was born. The early believers waited in Jerusalem for heavenly power, and God answered their prayers. The population of Jerusalem was around thirty thousand at this time, so when Scripture says about three thousand people put their faith in Jesus that day, this was about 10 percent of the city (Acts 2:41). That, obviously, is a *fantastic* response to the good news!

But I don't think God's heart is satisfied with 10 percent. What about the other 90 percent? God wants all of us. How can we start to step into *His* faith for our cities?

There is no city so dark that His light cannot penetrate it. There is no city so "untouchable" that it can resist God's love.

With the mind of Christ, let's start to believe nothing is impossible—even for our city. As our hearts are saturated with this hope, our prayers become effective and aligned with God's love in every possible way (see Jas. 5:16).

Intercession Point

> Ask God to help you believe in faith that no city is beyond His touch or influence—including yours. Pray with an open and believing heart, ready to see the impossible occur in this city you love.

Chapter 2

CHOOSING UNCONDITIONAL LOVE FOR YOUR CITY

I ministered in the rougher downtown area of Santa Cruz for years. After the birth of my first child, I bought a house in what I thought was a nice neighborhood because I wanted my young family to grow up in a safe place.

As I got to know my neighbors, I discovered the one on the right was a practicing witch, the ones on the left were dealing drugs, and the house in the back was a major party house.

Okay. Change of plans.

I began to pray for them, and I felt like God said He was going to change their lives. But a couple of years later, I stood on my balcony and watched as one of my neighbors made a drug deal right in front of my house.

"I thought You said You were going to take care of this," I complained to God. "What are You doing?"

I sensed Him reply, "I am going to love them and show them mercy, just like I did with you."

As God's love for them pierced my heart, I felt convicted because of how much mercy I had received myself. I realized I needed to realign my heart with God's love for my neighbors.

Paul understood this concept when he asked, "Don't you see how wonderfully kind, tolerant, and patient God is with you? Does this mean nothing to you? Can't you see that his kindness is intended to turn you from your sin?" (Rom. 2:4).

To be honest, for a long time I thought the answer to my prayer was for the police to show up and arrest my neighbors. But eventually God told me, "Stop trying to be Me and start loving Me."

When I fall into judgment, I create high standards—standards I *assume* mirror God's. But when I start to love Jesus, when I really start to love Him, I begin to love broken people who are not repentant. I begin to have hope for their lives as if they were already walking with Jesus.

> Dear friends, let us continue to love one another, for love comes from God. Anyone who loves is a child of God and knows God. But anyone who does not love does not know God, for God is love.
>
> 1 John 4:7-8

ADVOCATE

My heart's desire is to be a friend and representative of God and to know His lovingkindness in radical ways. As I pursue having His heart for others, His perspective of love changes me forever.

God is calling us to release His love and mercy toward our cities as we worship Him and follow His leading.

Bitterness Cuts Us Off from Hope

After years of drug and alcohol abuse, I began to surrender my heart to Jesus. I moved from Southern California to Santa Cruz to get a fresh start, and over the course of a year, my life began to be transformed. I became eager, nearly anxious, to share this good news with anyone who would listen. If God could change me, He could impact anyone.

I began to share the gospel in downtown Santa Cruz, where many people didn't listen to me. But I wasn't overly discouraged in those early days, because my focus was on those who did listen and were getting healed, saved, and set free. I saw a lot of fruit back then, and I think it was because I didn't have any judgments about the city and the people who lived there.

The attitude of older believers caught me off guard. After trying to reach the city for years, they had become discouraged and eventually stopped their efforts. *What?* I didn't get it. Why were they no longer doing what I was so excited about doing?

But slowly I began to understand. My faith for the city dimmed, and disappointment crept in, replacing the hope that used to flood my heart. I even got to the point of ridiculing other believers. When people with more faith than I moved into town, I quietly mocked their bright hope for what God was going to do in the city. "Oh really, huh? God's going to change the city because you're here? Great." They were full of dreams and vision, while I was discouraged and weighed down with doubt and criticism.

Somehow along the way, I began to store up all the rejection I'd experienced over the years and take it personally, which caused me to grow bitter toward the very city I loved. How could I intercede for a city when I was leaking toxic bitterness toward it?

I needed a personal renewal that would replace my stone-cold heart with one full of love (Ezek. 36:26).

Choosing Love Even When You're Rejected

There's a powerful story in the Old Testament where a king sent troops to arrest the prophet Elijah. Elijah said to the captain who had come to arrest him, "If I am a man of God . . . may fire come down from heaven and kill you and your men!" And that's exactly what happened. Fire fell from heaven and killed the soldiers (2 Kings 1:10).

Hundreds of years later, two of Jesus's disciples obviously knew this story very well. When a Samaritan village rejected Jesus, James and John went to Him and said, "Lord, we've got an idea—do You want us to call fire down from heaven to destroy them?" (See Luke 9.)

How many times I have dreamed of having a missile launcher mounted to my car when someone cuts me off in traffic! Probably all of us know what the sting of rejection or injustice feels like. When we know we have been wronged, we want to see God judge the situation with overwhelming power.

But fire from heaven was not the answer Jesus wanted. He sharply criticized the disciples' attitude toward the Samaritan village. The people had rejected the incredible gift God Himself was offering them—it was a big deal. Yet Jesus kept a loving attitude toward them. He knew exactly what they were saying no to, but He didn't allow the rejection to become bitterness in His heart.

That needs to be our response as well. In Luke 9:5 Jesus gave great advice on how to keep a loving attitude: "Wherever people don't welcome you, leave that town." For me, this means that whenever I'm rejected, I can choose to let it go. I have a hard time letting things go, but I've learned I need to "destroy every proud obstacle" that keeps me from "knowing God" (2 Cor. 10:5). My frustration with people who don't measure up to my self-righteous standards can keep me from loving them.

If we're going to reach our cities with God's unconditional love, we need to learn to forgive people and move forward with them. We can't hold grudges and bitterness toward a city and at the same time intercede for its salvation.

> Understand this, my dear brothers and sisters: You must all be quick to listen, slow to speak, and slow to get angry. Human anger does not produce the righteousness God desires. So get rid of all the filth and evil in your lives, and humbly accept the word God has planted in your hearts, for it has the power to save your souls.
>
> James 1:19-21

This kind of "human" anger is the Greek word *orge*, which basically means deep anger because of bad experiences.[1] When we're dealing with *orge*, we tend to reject others first to guard ourselves from further disappointment.

Many of us desire good, perfectly reasonable things for our city like the elimination of crime, corruption, and poverty. We know those things are wrong, and they hurt people we care about. When these reasonable desires for peace and health go unfulfilled, negativity can start building up in our hearts, which causes our minds to become "cloudy." Solomon put it like this: "Hope deferred makes the heart sick, but a dream fulfilled is a tree of life" (Prov. 13:12).

I want to see revival in every city and salvation in every person I connect with. When this doesn't happen, if I'm not careful, I can start to allow myself to get frustrated and angry. My desire is a good desire—but its lack of fulfillment does not produce good fruit inside me (Matt. 12:33-35).

---

1 Strong's Greek #3709.

In every situation, I want to produce good fruit that grows naturally within my heart. This means I need to allow Jesus to *overwhelm* my heart with His love and forgiveness. That's the good soil that produces good fruit in my life.

Walking in Salvation Daily

As a new homeowner, I was introduced to restrictive building codes and obnoxious neighbors. I paid high taxes, heard stories about corrupt officials, listened to people's complaints, and watched news stories that depressed me and hurled stones against my hope for my city. During this time, I also worked as an associate pastor of a charismatic church that didn't get much support from other conservative churches in the area. They really weren't all that interested in helping us out.

So I grew more and more cynical until one day I came face to face with my hopeless attitude—I met a pastor who was so excited about what God was going to do. He believed God had given him a vision for revival, and he was actively pursuing this calling.

When I heard his dreams for the city, my heart did not respond with hope. I had worked for years and hadn't seen what he was talking about, so this was my attitude: "Yeah, good luck with that."

A few years later, I was spiritually burned out, and bitterness had rooted itself within my spirit. I'd allowed my heart to be influenced by negative circumstances and had let go of the simple truth James shared: "Humbly accept the word God has planted in your hearts, for it has the power to save your souls" (Jas. 1:21). That was what my soul needed—it needed to be "saved" or made whole again through the simple and powerful love of Jesus. My hope and excitement for people needed to be revived.

Living Prayers

Our attitudes are powerful. If we allow them to fill up with anger and frustration, we won't shine very brightly. We can still pray—but our lives will not *be* a prayer, which is what God wants. It's possible for our whole lives, every part of us and how we live, to reflect His light and love to the world.

"Those who are peacemakers will plant seeds of peace and reap a harvest of righteousness" (Jas. 3:18). If I'm going to be a revivalist who carries hope for my city, I need to make peace with anything that has hurt me in my past. I need to allow God to do a deep work of healing inside me and empower me with His grace to forgive the very people who tell me, "I'm not interested," over and over again.

I know what it feels like to have anger and bitterness course through my veins. My heart rate goes up, I can't focus, and it's difficult to sleep. It's like drinking poison that one day will lead to the death of my hope.

But I also know what it feels like to be overwhelmed with the goodness of Jesus. My entire body and mind begin to rest in an indescribable peace, and I feel power flowing through my spirit. Nothing seems impossible to me, and even loving my neighbor who annoys me becomes a joy.

ADVOCATE

If I want to see my city transformed with God's grace, I need to be radically changed myself, so I can become a *living prayer* for people.

In the Old Testament, Abraham integrated God's heart of mercy and became a peacemaker who wanted people to live. When he learned God intended to destroy two wicked cities, Abraham's first reaction was to plead for mercy for the righteous people who might be living there (Gen. 18:24-25).

God could not have agreed more. He would have spared the city for only ten innocent people (v. 32). Can you see how much He *loves* mercy?

Many years later, God asked Ezekiel, "Do you think that I like to see wicked people die?" There can be no doubt of the Lord's heart because He answered His question Himself: "Of course not! I want them to turn from their wicked ways and live" (Ez. 18:23).

Abraham and Ezekiel both knew God's desire to see sinners live, be set free, and begin to thrive as new children of God.

Praying for Your City

God's heart is *always* for restoration and forgiveness, and He wants to develop that same heart of mercy within us. When we encounter His love, our hearts come alive. We all need the presence of Jesus to activate our true selves so we can shine His love and light. I want to carry God's heart in all things, because it causes people who are stuck to *wake up* and it produces good fruit within my city.

Jesus knew full well that He would be falsely accused and killed in Jerusalem. Yet He said anyway:

> O Jerusalem, Jerusalem, the city that kills the prophets and stones God's messengers! How often I have wanted to gather your children together as a hen protects her chicks beneath her wings, but you wouldn't let me.
>
> Luke 13:34

Even to those who wanted to kill Him, Jesus responded with love and forgiveness. He wanted to *embrace* His enemies, even though He knew they wouldn't receive His love.

That's the kind of heart we can cultivate as well. Let's accept God's hope and mercy and embrace the cities we live in.

Intercession Point

> Ask God to open your heart to see how wonderfully kind, tolerant, and patient He is with you. Understand He feels the same way toward the "worst" person in your city. How can you pray for that person today—the one you think is doing the most damage or living in the most rebellion? As you're praying, speak words of kindness over them.

Chapter 3
THE EXCHANGE OF INTERCESSION

One morning I was at the church organizing canned foods for an outreach when another church member stopped by and introduced me to the plumber who was going to replace a broken toilet.

I realized this was the same plumber who had incorrectly installed a dishwasher in my house. The thing had leaked and caused hundreds of dollars in damage to my floors. I'd tried to call the plumber several times, but he never bothered getting back to me.

When I saw the same plumber at my church, a wave of resentment rolled through me, but I could tell my anger was not from God. I asked Him to help me with my irritation and also to help me forgive this man, so I could stay civilized and polite.

A little while later, I went to the pantry and flicked the light switch. But nothing happened.

So I replaced the bulbs and tried again. Still nothing. The room remained dark.

I pulled the bulbs out and tried them in a lamp to make sure they were good—they were, but when I took them back to the pantry and replaced them in the sockets, they still didn't work.

What is this? I wondered, perplexed. Sensing something was amiss, I tuned my mind and heart to listen to God.

The plumber immediately came to mind. I knew I still held a grudge toward him.

"God, please forgive me," I said without much passion and tried the switch again.

The lights didn't work.

I felt the Lord say to my spirit, "If you truly forgive, the light will work."

I knew I was busted and finally took the situation seriously. Breathing a deep sigh, I let go of the plumber's debt. I completely released it and felt faith and assurance inside me. This time when I flicked the switch, the lights came on. I stood there in awe at the Lord's teaching.

Later when I walked outside, I saw the plumber working by his truck. I said hello without any anger or resentment. I wished him only the best and in my heart blessed him sincerely. This kind of forgiveness doesn't come easily for me—but it's amazing what God can do with a light switch.

ADVOCATE

As followers of Jesus who care about the people around us, our job is to assume the role of light as we stand in dark places. If we're going to be light, we need to get out of the way and let Jesus have *His* way in our thoughts.

> For God, who said, "Let there be light in the darkness," has made this light shine in our hearts so we could know the glory of God that is seen in the face of Jesus Christ.
> 2 Corinthians 4:6

Anger and frustration dim the light seen in the face of Jesus. Only in humility can I represent God's heart to a broken world.

A Beautiful Exchange

When Jesus was in anguish the night before the crucifixion, He went to an olive grove to pray.

> He went on a little farther and bowed with his face to the ground, praying, "My Father! If it is possible, let this cup of suffering be taken away from me. Yet I want your will to be done, not mine."
> Matthew 26:39

The word *prayer* here in the Greek is *proseúxomai*, which means to exchange your wishes.[1] It literally means to "switch" your ideas for God's as He gives you the faith you need. In other words, the lifestyle of an intercessor looks like constantly turning to God to see what He is saying

---
1 Strong's Greek #4336.

about you, someone else, or a situation. You and I get to walk in God's shoes and see things from His perspective as we intercede for our cities and release faith-filled prayers.

When we deal with irritating people or circumstances, that's when we truly get to see the reality of *proseúxomai*. It's prayer that changes *us,* the people who are praying. Who intercedes when things are going great and they feel blessed? Honestly, that usually isn't when I start praying hard. Intercession goes way deeper than eloquent words. It involves changing our attitude and surrendering our mind, heart, and soul to God. It is the highest expression of repentance when we're struggling with anger and resentment, which are full of judgments and accusations.

True intercession empowers us to release a heartfelt plea for mercy and blessings for our enemies or anyone else we perceive to be a problem. This interaction with God—the exchange of our thoughts—is the heart of intercession. If we're going to be a light in our city, we need to come into alignment with God's heart for the city. This means surrendering other people's sins and faults and declaring we want *His* will alone to be done.

The apostle Paul dealt with a lot of people who tried to stop the momentum of love and grace God had given him to express. Sometimes God actually sent these people Paul's way to test the apostle's heart. Paul endured "insults, hardships, persecutions, and troubles" (2 Cor. 12:10), and he called the instigators *thorns in his flesh* (v. 7). We probably would use different language today, but we can tell these people were really troubling to Paul and distracted his focus.

ADVOCATE

Thorns may be small, but when we've been insulted and persecuted, that "thorn" can feel like a sword in the back. It drains all our energy and can twist our attitude toward the people around us.

When a constant irritation gets under our skin, we usually become defensive and then react. But God wants us to respond with grace and love so we can bring peace into any situation. He wants us to learn to guard our hearts so our first reaction is to seek His heart for the people and situations around us.

In response to these problem people, Paul begged God three different times to take them away. He pleaded like an innocent person in front of a judge. I can imagine him saying, "But, God—I don't deserve this. Send fire down from heaven and remove these annoying people from my life!"

Pride keeps us from seeing from God's perspective. We can truly intercede only when we are empowered to recognize that He has a plan for *everyone*, even our enemies.

Recently I bought a house and wanted to build some structures in my backyard. To get approval from the housing association, I first needed to inform my neighbors about my plans and give them time to voice any concerns.

One neighbor let me know that several years ago, another neighbor had severely hassled his construction plans. So he told me he wasn't going to make it easy for me to get approval—because, apparently, that was the only way the situation would be "fair."

I couldn't believe this guy's attitude. I allowed myself to get extremely annoyed and brought my case before God again and again.

I felt like God asked me, "What do you really want?"

"I want this guy to sell his house and move away!" I replied.

"Okay," God answered. "You can ask for that."

So I began to pray and pray for this neighbor to move, rationalizing that it would be the best for him and me.

But then one morning, I felt like God told me, "Now I want you to pray that your neighbor would stay and not move."

What? Hesitantly I tried to obey. For about half a day, I prayed my neighbor would stay and not move.

Later that day, I sensed God saying to me, "Now I want you to pray that your neighbor would sell his house and move."

Yes! With excitement, I again started praying for my neighbor to move.

But as I prayed this way, I began to feel a darkness in my spirit. I instantly knew something was wrong with my desire to pray that prayer, and I realized I had no empathy in my heart for my neighbor. God opened my eyes to see how that prayer was not in His heart.

ADVOCATE

God doesn't abandon cities or people. Instead, He continually has a plan that is filled with hope and a future. I didn't care about my neighbor. I wanted to see him as a problem—but that was not how God wanted me to see him.

I began to repent for my insensitive response. Since that time, I've been trying to bless my neighbor, hoping he'll embrace God's love and receive healing from his past hurts and disappointments.

Anger can be a tempting emotion that makes us feel powerful and in control. Paul wanted the people who were annoying him just to vanish because—at least, this is how *I* would respond—he couldn't control what they were doing, and this made him aware of his weakness.

> Three different times I begged the Lord to take it away. Each time he said, "My grace is all you need. My power works best in weakness."
> 2 Corinthians 12:8-9

Being angry and condemning the world around us makes us feel powerful. When we're "locked" within that sense of power, giving it up to trust God's ways instead can make us feel weak. Many of us struggle to believe that mercy really does triumph over judgment (Jas. 2:13). I am way too familiar with anger and the desire for a reason to be angry.

The temptation to feel angry and powerful destroys the intercession of mercy God wants us to walk in. He wants us to give Him our frustrations and, in exchange, be filled with His compassion toward everyone, including annoying neighbors who really have no right to make our lives miserable.

> Keep watch and pray, so that you will not give in to temptation. For the spirit is willing, but the body is weak!
> Matthew 26:41

Seeing from God's Perspective

King David had some crazy obstacles thrown at him as he tried to follow God's will for his life. His circumstances weren't always easy, but he wrote songs to help him enter God's presence and be transformed by His love.

In Psalm 108 we see the "exchange" of David's thoughts for God's thoughts:

> My heart is confident in you, O God;
> no wonder I can sing your praises with all my heart!
> …For your unfailing love is higher than the heavens.
> Your faithfulness reaches to the clouds…
> May your glory shine over all the earth.
>
> Now rescue your beloved people.
> Answer and save us by your power.
> Psalm 108:1-6

ADVOCATE

David started with personal thanksgiving and, from that place, moved into seeing God's mercy for him. As he saw God's mercy for him personally, he started to intercede and ended up releasing God's light to shine over all the earth. As he worshiped the Lord, his heart was transformed into that of a revivalist, one who wanted everyone to experience God's presence the way he did.

Here's a really simple way to apply this idea. I do not wake up well. When someone wishes me a good morning, my attitude is like, "What could *possibly* be good right now?"

But over time I have come to realize this is not who I really am. Jesus has eternally transformed me, and God has a great plan for my life, no matter how tired or depressed I may feel at times. I need to guard my heart from my own negative perspectives and be careful about how I judge or criticize what my life looks like.

> Guard your heart above all else,
> for it determines the course of your life.
>
> Avoid all perverse talk;
> stay away from corrupt speech.
>
> Proverbs 4:23-24

The Hebrew words for "perverse" and "corrupt" both mean crooked or to depart from the path God intends.[2] So the first thing I need is love—both for myself and for the world. When I "change lanes" and start taking the wrong path of anger and frustration, I lose my ability to release His mercy.

---
2 Strong's Hebrew #3891.

Therefore, it is vital I go to Jesus and see His perspective, what He's thinking, for myself and then also for my city. Guarding my heart is the door that allows God's love to flow through me and into the world.

> Anyone who believes in me may come and drink! For the Scriptures declare, "Rivers of living water will flow from his heart."
> John 7:38

Those Who Don't Deserve It

Jonah's story is a great example of how easy it is to become judgmental toward an entire city and not be in agreement with God's heart.

God sent this guy to Nineveh—an enemy city—to deliver a warning so the people would turn from their hopeless mentality and wicked ways and receive His plan for them. Jonah reluctantly delivered God's message and, just as Jonah predicted, the whole city of Nineveh repented. They completely changed and turned to God.

When Jonah saw this, he didn't respond positively, which shows his heart wasn't aligned with God's vision for the city. Instead he started complaining:

> Didn't I say before I left home that you would do this, Lord? That is why I ran away to Tarshish! I knew that you are a merciful and compassionate God, slow to get angry and filled with unfailing love. You are eager to turn back from destroying people.
> Jonah 4:2

ADVOCATE

Jonah saw the corruption that lived and breathed in Nineveh, and he didn't think the people deserved God's mercy. He basically said, "Lord, it would be better for these people to die in their sins because that's what they deserve. Don't save them, God. There is nothing worth saving here!"

But that wasn't God's heart. He saw the city's wickedness even more clearly than Jonah did, and the response of His heart was love.

Are we quick to forgive national or city leaders who are corrupt? Or do we write them off like Jonah did? Honestly, I can relate to Jonah's mindset more quickly than I can God's. This is still an area where I need a lot of help.

Jonah's story is crazy. He tried to escape God's plan and ended up on a ship in the middle of a terrifying storm. Realizing the storm existed because of him—because he wasn't doing what God had ordered—he told the crew to throw him overboard so they would live. When they did what he requested, the storm stopped. Just like that.

Jonah, meanwhile, was swallowed by a huge fish, and he lived inside the fish for three days before he repented and God saved him.

After this experience, Jonah clearly knew the mercy and grace of God, His miracle-working power, and how He turns *impossibility* into *possibility*—and yet Jonah still had an issue with sharing the mercy he'd received. He was brought back from certain death, but he still had no compassion toward people who struggled with the same rebellion he did.

When we're honest with ourselves, most of us have to admit we often respond like Jonah. All of us have our "favorite" corrupt city, political group, or sinful lifestyle we enjoy talking about and being frustrated with. It is likely God is calling us to the very people we hate. He wants to reverse our anger and empower us to experience freedom from the poison slowly killing our hearts.

God is so full of compassion and mercy for people! He asked Jonah to see His side of the story and helped him open his eyes to a new perspective. "Nineveh has more than 120,000 people living in spiritual darkness, not to mention all the animals. Shouldn't I feel sorry for such a great city?" (Jon. 4:11).

God wants to see whole cities impacted with His love and mercy. We can partner with His heart and live a lifestyle of compassion toward the very people who don't "deserve" the gift He wants to give them.

Praying for Your City

A few years ago, I asked God to show me what to do that day.

I felt Him say, "When you go to leave the house, your question should not be 'What am I to do today?' But 'Who am I today?' When you know who you are, then you will automatically know what to do."

ADVOCATE

The heart of intercession begins with remembering who we are. God constantly speaks encouraging and empowering words to remind us we're loved, accepted, and secure.

The prophet Daniel knew who he was, and because of his calm trust in God, he was able to influence many nations. When his enemies purposefully created a law meant to destroy him, he didn't get angry. He just went home and surrendered his thoughts in exchange for God's thoughts.

> But when Daniel learned that the law had been signed, he went home and knelt down as usual in his upstairs room, with its windows open toward Jerusalem. He prayed three times a day, just as he had always done, giving thanks to his God.
> Daniel 6:10

He daily exchanged what was on his mind for what God was thinking, and this habit enabled him to walk in a supernatural peace.[3] Even when his enemies succeeded and had him thrown to the lions, he didn't panic.

> Very early the next morning, the king got up and hurried out to the lions' den. When he got there, he called out in anguish, "Daniel, servant of the living God! Was your God, whom you serve so faithfully, able to rescue you from the lions?"

---

[3] How can we live in supernatural peace? Philippians 4:6-7 shows the way.

> Daniel answered, "Long live the king! My God sent his angel to shut the lions' mouths so that they would not hurt me, for I have been found innocent in his sight. And I have not wronged you, Your Majesty."
>
> Daniel 6:19-22

Look at Daniel's attitude here. He cared for the king he faithfully served—the same king who had signed into law an edict that would cause Daniel to be arrested and, or so the plan was, killed in a brutal way.

But Daniel didn't focus on the unjustness of his situation. He loved his king, and it was in his heart to see the king live a long and blessed life.

That is the kind of heart we need to have for our leaders as well. A heart that doesn't focus on what they're doing wrong and how it will affect us, but one that loves them and wishes the best for them. In this way, we will be able to powerfully intercede for our cities and national leaders so they will see God is real and good. May the mercy of God fill our hearts for every person in our cities.

Intercession Point

> Ask God to fill your mind and heart with faith to see your entire city radically transformed by His love. Ask Him to help you pray for your city leaders the way Daniel did.

Chapter 4

WHEN BLESSING IS UNDESERVED

Even though my father's health was growing worse, he didn't want to go to the doctor and find out what was wrong. He believed that if he got checked out, it would be bad news, so he chose to ignore his increasing symptoms.

By the time he finally did go to see someone, the doctor immediately recommended an emergency double-bypass heart surgery. "If you'd waited any longer, you certainly would have died from a heart attack," the doctor said.

When I heard the doctor's report, anxiety paralyzed me. With the surgery scheduled for the following morning, I visited the little chapel our church had set up for prayer and intercession. The moment I sat down in the chair, pain and the fear of losing my dad overwhelmed me. It felt like a heavy cloud filled my mind to the point I couldn't even think. Tears streamed down my face as I imagined the worst possible outcome.

Others in the chapel were praying or quietly soaking in God's presence. My attempts at prayer were interrupted when I heard a gurgling sound behind me—someone had fallen asleep on the floor and was snoring.

I tried to ignore it at first, but this guy was loud. The ridiculousness of the situation struck me, and I started laughing. The more I laughed, the better I felt, so I just sat there and allowed the joy to flow through my heart.

It was like a wind came and blew away the heaviness from my heart, and I began to see in the spirit. As I looked with my spiritual eyes, I saw a picture of my dad healthy and full of life, and I started to believe he could make a full recovery. My perspective completely transformed, and I knew I had exchanged my dark, personal thoughts for God's prophetic insight.

The surgery was a complete success, and I got to experience firsthand the restoration of my hope.

My prayers for my dad were answered that day in the chapel, but I knew my faith didn't come from me. The *only* way I was able to step into faith at all was because I intentionally made the decision to see what God saw.

Many of us think of great faith as something a person attains only after years of meditating in a monastery or performing great miracles like Moses did. But I've learned that faith is a *gift* that can be received with a childlike heart. The key to believing for a city or an individual is positioning our hearts in surrender to God, where we give Him all our previous thoughts and replace our attitude with His.

Persuaded by God

> Are any of you sick? You should call for the elders of the church to come and pray over you, anointing you with oil in the name of the Lord. Such a prayer offered in faith will heal the sick, and the Lord will make you well.
>
> James 5:14-15

Life-transforming prayers are offered "in faith," which means that without faith, the prayer would be just words.

I don't want to squander my life, my heart, and my emotions by pushing them in a direction that doesn't produce good fruit. The Greek word for "faith" in James 5 is *pistis*, which means to be persuaded.[1] A child can easily be persuaded, and most of us categorize this tendency as immaturity or weakness. Someone who is naïve or gullible can be manipulated and taken advantage of.

In my pride, I like to think I know what I'm doing and am a strong person who doesn't need help, but I've discovered that's actually a deceptive attitude. When that's my mindset, I tend to think the facts point only to one logical conclusion, and I can miss the supernatural answers that are seen only through childlike persuasion—that is, through faith. By nature, I am highly logical and love it when picture frames hang level on a wall. I don't like to lean on others for help, and I take pride in being self-sufficient. But this kind of attitude doesn't align with how God created me to thrive. In order to really enjoy God's love, peace, and

---

[1] Strong's Greek #4102.

joy, I've discovered I need to surrender my individualistic reliance on myself.

We enter the kingdom of God through childlike faith. This faith is never produced through effort or knowledge, but we receive it as we simply and guilelessly connect with God. He wants to expand our minds so we're able to see our connection and need for His input in our lives. When we struggle to believe and see the good in our world, He wants us to see with His eyes that are full of light and hope.

The more I allow my heart *to be persuaded* by what God is saying, the more I'm able to receive His thoughts and follow Him instead of my fact-driven, humanly logical mind. The more submitted my heart is, the more I see what God is doing.

When Blessing Is Undeserved

When I was twenty-two and very young in my walk with Jesus, I started a discipleship house where I lived with six new believers who used to be homeless. We spent most of our time helping at a downtown mission that served the street kids and homeless in Santa Cruz.

One night at the mission, we were singing songs and worshiping together when someone started pounding on the front door.

"Four teenagers were just in a car accident," a homeless man told us. "Could you help them?"

ADVOCATE

When the teenagers arrived at the house, we discovered they didn't actually want our help. They balked when we offered to take them to the hospital. (Later we learned the car was stolen.)

Everyone pitched in to take care of the injured. We set up cots so they could lie down, and we made some popcorn. One guy was especially hurt. He could barely move his neck and his knee was severely banged up. None of us knew how to help these kids from a medical standpoint, so once they were settled, we returned to worship.

As I was worshiping, God gave me an idea: I should pray for healing for the guy who was in the most pain. So I went over to his cot, and as I prayed for him, I felt the presence of God flowing powerfully through my hand into his body.

"Do you feel any relief from the pain?" I asked.

"No," he replied. "I don't feel anything."

After praying for several minutes, I started to get confused because nothing changed. I was so convinced that God was doing something, but this kid didn't feel any different. Eventually I gave up and went back to worshiping with my housemates.

The hour grew late, and we shut everything down and started to pack up the car. But as we were pulling out of the driveway, someone ran up to the window and started jumping up and down right outside our car.

It was so dark that I couldn't see who it was at first, but then I realized it was the guy I had prayed for. He was swinging his head around and showing us he was no longer in any pain. God, in His mercy, had completely healed the boy's body, even though this kid was a thief on the run.

The next day we purchased bus tickets to send all the teenagers back to their homes in Texas. A couple of weeks later, I got a call from the mother of the guy who was healed—she wanted to know what really happened with her son.

As we talked, I found out she was a Christian, but she believed God didn't heal or do miracles anymore. She had a hard time believing her son had been badly injured—because he arrived home in perfect health. Yet she could not deny that *something* had happened. She was shocked because her son who had been on a rebellious path was now reading his Bible every day and wanted to become a pastor.

For many years whenever I thought about this story, I felt pride because of God's amazing healing miracle and the transformative repentance that resulted. But a problem arose because I focused only on what God *did*, not on His heart for those four teenagers. He recently convicted me about this because honestly, I didn't see that teenage criminal as worthy of his healing—I just saw a young punk who stole a car and led others into chaos and pain. Even though I expected God to heal him, I was surprised when the healing actually occurred. Considering the circumstances, the boy's actions did not justify the amazing grace and mercy he received.

I witnessed God's compassion that night. I saw it firsthand—but I did not allow Him to transform my judgmental mindset that wanted to decide who was "worthy" and who was "not worthy." I even felt the joy of God's presence flowing through me, but my critical mindset did not allow me to change and *absorb* His love for these kids. They had stolen a car! How did God fail to notice all their mistakes? What about "Thou shalt honor your mother and father"? Or "Thou shalt not steal"?

It is difficult to let go of a performance mindset because we subconsciously enjoy the power and control it gives us over others. But God has called us to turn continually from our pride and discover His heart for all people. He wants us to be able to share the gospel, pray for healing, and—most important—be genuinely loving and merciful toward others. Our job is to "love mercy and to walk humbly" (Mic. 6:8). I cannot love mercy while holding on to a rulebook that allows me to be the judge with the power to decide who wins and who doesn't.

If our goal is to be light to the people around us, we need to weed out even the smallest judgments from our heart. If our mindset does not agree with God's heart for people, we risk misrepresenting His message.

All of us naturally like to give to those who most deserve it or who truly need a blessing. Most of us don't understand when people receive above and beyond what they already have or are blessed more than we feel they deserve. Yet that is the nature of heaven. In His story about the servants and the coins, Jesus exposed how we like to argue with God's perspective:

> The king ordered, "Take the money from this servant, and give it to the one who has ten pounds."
>
> "But, master," they said, "he already has ten pounds!"
>
> Luke 19:24-25

It shouldn't surprise us to discover God doesn't think like we do, but we still like to argue our point of view. I argue with Him a lot—but I also try to learn and listen for His heart. Sometimes His mercy frustrates me to no end. I don't always want to follow what He's doing, but I know there's grace for me to figure things out. It's okay.

In our culture, people celebrate and honor soldiers who have suffered and sacrificed for our freedom. We also love generous people who give freely and serve the community well. Cornelius is a perfect example of someone who, in my mind, earned blessings and favor from God. I imagine his neighbors and friends rejoiced with him when he received a visit from the apostle Peter—because Cornelius deserved it.

> In Caesarea there lived a Roman army officer named Cornelius, who was a captain

ADVOCATE

> of the Italian Regiment. He was a devout, God-fearing man, as was everyone in his household. He gave generously to the poor and prayed regularly to God.
>
> Acts 10:1-2

This guy deserved to be honored. But what is our attitude when someone who doesn't live an exemplary lifestyle is blessed just as extravagantly—if not *more* extravagantly?

Sometimes we have a hard time understanding why God would "waste" His time blessing delinquent criminals who don't deserve His favor. Yet that is what God did in Scripture again and again:

> But the other criminal protested, "Don't you fear God even when you have been sentenced to die? We deserve to die for our crimes, but this man hasn't done anything wrong." Then he said, "Jesus, remember me when you come into your Kingdom."
>
> And Jesus replied, "I assure you, today you will be with me in paradise."
>
> Luke 23:40-43

Jesus was able to put aside any thoughts about this man's actions and declare he was going to live like a king for eternity. This criminal essentially triumphed over death with *one moment* of humility and trust.

I wish I could have seen the faces of those standing nearby

listening to this conversation. This guy was *crucified*—he knew exactly what he'd done wrong, and he freely stated he deserved this horrific death. Did Jesus completely ignore everything the man said except for that final sentence? Instead of focusing on the man's many sins, He spoke out loud what His Father was doing in the moment and did not allow His human mind to interfere.

If we're going to be the light of the world, we need to learn to replace our judgmental mindsets more and more quickly, so we can release blessing into every situation. Even to those people who deserve God's favor the least. If my prayers for a person are full of my own judgments and criticisms, I hope those prayers are never answered. Any prayer I pray that is motivated by my selfish desires contradicts God's heart.

James addressed selfish desires when he wrote, "And even when you ask, you don't get it because your motives are all wrong—you want only what will give you pleasure" (4:3). It's possible for us to get wrapped up in prayers that are focused on what *we* want, not what God wants. We can spend a whole lot of time insisting God should do what we want Him to do—what would give us pleasure in the moment. You know what would give me pleasure when someone cuts me off in traffic? That missile launcher I was telling you about. I am thankful God ignores these selfish desires.

As He proved in my story about the car thief, God sometimes answers our prayers because He loves to help people, not because He approves of our motivation in the moment.

How He Loves

One time I flew across the country and drove deep into the woods of Pennsylvania to attend a National Rainbow Gathering with a friend. This is an event where thousands of earth-loving people camp together and talk about their message of world peace. My friend and I went there to be a light, to make friends, and to help people see God's love for them.

I never know how to connect with people, but I've discovered that if I don't get out and try, I won't learn. So I always try to have an attitude that allows me to keep learning and stay dependent on God's guidance. Staying humble is a key to discovering His heart for people.

One night during the event, my friend and I walked to the center of camp and started singing. Being the more experienced musician, my friend picked a few Bob Dylan songs as well as some worship songs that weren't as well known, because we wanted to stay under the radar and not overtly conflict with the event's New Age focus.

We were singing "How He Loves" by John Mark McMillan when a guy who clearly wasn't sober strolled over and stood next to us. When we finished the song, he asked us to sing it again, and as we started back up, to our surprise, he joined in and knew every word.

"I often sing this song at my home church," he told us later.

What? When I found out this guy attended a church, my heart instantly began to judge him. I felt disgusted as I thought about this "Christian" being drunk and, from my perspective, not living a great example. Didn't he know the other people here needed him? And they needed him to be a better example than this.

As I glared at the guy, I took a breath and realized my inner frustrations weren't helping anything. So instead, I decided to listen to what God was saying about this man. I'd recently heard some teachings about prophetically calling out the "gold" in people instead of just pointing out the dirt. As I searched for the gold in this man, I heard God say, "This man is a leader, and many people have not seen his potential."

I saw a picture of a stone colonnade or pillar—like something found at an ancient ruin in Greece. This is a common picture for me when I pray for leaders who are able to stand strong and support others.

The Spirit of God overwhelmed my angry judgment, and before I could stop myself, I started sharing with this man what I knew God was saying about him. I spoke with confidence, knowing in my spirit the words were perfectly true, even though my mind was confused and didn't think this guy deserved to be empowered this way.

The man broke down and began to cry. "I know I'm a leader," he said, but no one around him back in the "real world" could see his true identity and strengths. He was always overlooked.

So, at a New Age event, my friend and I prayed a blessing over this man so he could step into his calling as a leader.

As I felt God's heart of mercy rush through me, I could sense how different it was from my own heart in the moment. My mind was still not fully persuaded, and I felt a battle brewing within me because now I would have to let go of my critical and controlling mindset.

We need to shift our view of people away from a worldly position of performance to a forgiven and empowering perspective.

Peter was present when God the Father declared who Jesus is: "The voice from the majestic glory of God said to him, 'This is my dearly loved Son, who brings me great joy'" (2 Pet. 1:17). I think those words are played in the spiritual realm like a broken record—over and over and over again, not just toward Jesus but into every person's heart. God sees every individual the same way He sees His Son (Col. 1:22). If God embraces every person into His presence, how can I not do the same?

How often do we see people as "hidden" in Jesus? "Think about the things of heaven, not the things of earth. For you died to this life, and your real life is hidden with Christ in God" (Col. 3:2-3). If I don't see people from a perspective filled with hope, one where even the worst of sinners has a future, I am not being obedient to the call God has on my life.

Changing the Environment

When I was a new parent with two kids, I worked full time as an associate pastor and struggled to carry too many responsibilities and pressures. Sometimes I would bring my frustrations home and vent them toward my family.

One time after I'd calmed down from an angry outburst, I repented and then took a moment to listen to what God was saying about this ongoing problem.

He showed me a picture of my living room where my wife and kids were sitting. I watched myself step through the front door, and the floor turned blue. The scene repeated itself, but this time when I entered the room, the floor turned red. God explained the illustration, helping me see that when I entered the house with peace in my heart, the floor turned blue: a color full of peace. But when I entered the house with anger and frustration, the floor turned red: a color full of anger. He revealed to me that my heart influenced my environment, and everyone in my family could feel it and was affected by it. I realized I was not guarding my heart—this was the first time I really understood how much my attitude negatively affected my family.

This picture challenged me to release "blue" everywhere I go. Though I've failed at this many times, my heart comes alive when I'm able to bring God's peace into the atmosphere. Solomon wrote that our hearts determine the course of our lives (Prov. 4:23). A person's heart is extraordinarily powerful, and just as my heart had a direct result on the atmosphere within my home, it can also influence my city.

What would it feel like to walk through a city and release peace with every step? What if we could feel joy and hope every time we saw people?

I want to pursue the kind of lifestyle where a *transfer* is made, and my angry or bitter heart that releases death is replaced with God's love that breathes life. I want my judgmental criticisms to be overcome with heavenly hope. The world needs love that "is not irritable, and it keeps no record of being wronged" (1 Cor. 13:5).

God began drawing me into His arms long before I had a single thought about repenting and turning to Him. He wants us to carry that same attitude toward everyone, so we create an atmosphere that invites broken people to seek Him. What if our simple decision to be *kind* could turn the city we love toward God?

When I first started attending church, I would often get overwhelmed to the point of tears as I felt God's goodness during worship. I would just weep as I felt His love touch my heart. Then later that same day, I would smoke pot, get drunk, and be intimate with my girlfriend who lived with me. Every day I experienced God's acceptance and love—even when I was living an unhealthy lifestyle. This went on for months until God's patient voice led me to repent from these behaviors that were holding me back from the path He planned for me.

He never withheld His love from me then, and He still doesn't withhold it—even when I make mistakes or bad decisions. Why, then, do so many of us feel like we get to decide who deserves our love and blessings and who doesn't?

> But I say, love your enemies! Pray for those who persecute you! In that way, you will be acting as true children of your Father in heaven. For he gives his sunlight to both the evil and the good, and he sends rain on the just and the unjust alike.
>
> Matthew 5:44-45

God's light does not judge first—before it begins to shine. He sends His blessings on everyone, and we need to practice that same heart because we're His representatives.

Praying for Your City

> "Come now, let's settle this,"
> says the Lord.
> "Though your sins are like scarlet,
> I will make them as white as snow."
>
> Isaiah 1:18

Recently as I was praying for a city, I saw a picture in my mind's eye of the city covered in snow. This reminded me of the Old Testament conversation between God and Isaiah, and I knew God wanted me to see this entire city as completely forgiven and loved. However, when I saw this city covered in snow, my mind immediately wanted to argue. Surely this was too generous—these people couldn't, in their current state, warrant this level of grace and forgiveness from God.

My heart is often inflexible and in need of a "spiritual renaissance" in order to fully absorb God's lavish love for people.

> I will give you a new heart, and I will put a new spirit in you. I will take out your stony, stubborn heart and give you a tender, responsive heart.
>
> Ezekiel 36:26

Most of us have an urgent need for this kind of heart transplant if we're going to learn to love the world. We need to discover God's heart for people so we can truly intercede for a city. As Paul wrote, "For God was in Christ, reconciling the world to himself, no longer counting people's sins against them" (2 Cor. 5:19).

If we're going to learn to love a city like Jesus does, we need to see those people through eyes of hope and allow God to "replace" our hard heart with one that looks exactly like His.

Intercession Point

> Ask God to help you surrender any apprehension and mistrust you feel when you think about entire cities turning to Him. Ask Him to teach you how to release peace as you go to different places in your city.

Chapter 5
LOOKING AT THE WORLD THROUGH GOD'S EYES

When I moved away to attend college, my party lifestyle accelerated to full speed. The town drunks living on the street became my good friends and selling drugs became my new profession. After dropping out of college, I traveled around the East Coast following the Grateful Dead and was arrested for selling LSD. But the arrest didn't slow me down, and I continued my self-destructive rampage, even though I knew this lifestyle would eventually kill me.

One night in San Francisco, I watched as a guy turned blue from a heroin overdose and almost died right in front of me. I realized my life was headed the same direction, but I didn't know how to turn around.

Several months later, something odd happened. I was hitchhiking and, to my surprise, no one would stop and give me a ride. It was like they didn't even see me. I sat down on the side of the road and, for the first time in my life, seriously began to contemplate who I was and what I was doing.

I'd been on a destructive path since my mother passed away when I was sixteen. I had just turned nineteen and was a homeless, alcoholic drug dealer facing two years in jail for dealing LSD. To top it all off, my girlfriend had left me and I was dead broke.

That morning I'd gotten a ride with an old hippie who happened to be reading the Bible. When I asked him why he was reading that divisive book, he said, "I really enjoy reading the red words."

He dropped me off and, without any food and little water, I walked seven miles through a city to end up where I was now—sitting on the side of the road because no one would pick me up. As I reflected on my life, I slowly became desperate enough to ask God for help.

At the time, I didn't believe in a creator and had never tried to communicate with God. As I considered how to pray, the cartoon *Tom and Jerry* popped into my mind. I remembered how they would put their hands together and pray when they felt their lives were in danger. So, with very little faith, I put my hands together and said, "God, if You're there, I could really use a ride right now."

That *instant*, a car skidded to a stop right in front of me, and I stared at it, speechless. I realized this was a sign God really existed, but even more amazing to me was that out of the billions of people in the world, this God knew about my insignificant existence.

For years I'd believed a lie that God was too busy fixing world hunger or helping people in war zones and didn't have time for me. Believing I didn't matter gave me an excellent excuse to continue living for myself and not caring about the consequences. But once I understood Someone cared about me and was with me, I finally had to let go of the lies holding me back from my destiny.

After that simple answered prayer, I felt like a phone line was hooked up between God and me, and I continued to ask for help. For the first time, I felt like there was hope, which made me curious about the supernatural. Months later I asked Jesus to forgive me, and I felt God's Spirit reclaiming the broken pieces of my heart. The more of my life I gave to Him, the more I found myself becoming who I really was. My true self. Over the next year, I allowed God to come close and love me, personally, and my destructive lifestyle reversed.

After experiencing this kind of incredible freedom and peace, I knew Jesus could do this again with anybody. I constantly said to myself, "If God loves me and I could get saved, then God loves everybody." I began to share my testimony with anyone who would listen, and I met others who were hungry for God's presence and life-changing power. I eventually started a recovery discipleship school that helped people get rooted in their faith and set free from addictions.

The hope I received wasn't just for me but also for everyone around me. At times God's love flooded my heart, and I would be overwhelmed and start crying because I wanted to see people come to know Jesus like I did. The love and faith I received from God replaced the deep rejection, fears, and pain that used to live in my heart. The emotions that fueled my addictions no longer dominated me.

We are called to carry so much hope that it overflows from our hearts and literally changes the city we live in. Our hearts were designed to believe in people and have faith for a bright future. As Jesus said, "A good person produces good things from the treasury of a good heart…What you say flows from what is in your heart" (Luke 6:45). Solomon also strongly believed in the heart's potency and wrote a powerful word of wisdom when he said, "Guard your heart above all else, for it determines the course of your life" (Prov. 4:23).

All of us know we need a good diet and exercise in order to keep our bodies in great shape, but how often do we do a health check on what's flowing from our hearts? A heart full of anger, stress, and judgment will highjack destiny because we were designed for abundance. An abundant heart releases life and healing—fruit that lines up with God's heart.

God's Approval and Acceptance

> Stand your ground, putting on the belt of truth and the body armor of God's righteousness.
>
> Ephesians 6:14

Paul wrote those words to warriors who were risking their lives to reach people and protect them in their city. The body armor or breastplate protected a person's vital organs, especially the heart.

ADVOCATE

The word *righteousness* in Greek is *dikaiosuné* and describes a powerful judicial declaration such as a verdict of guilt or innocence in a courtroom.[1] The verdict of heaven's court is simple—everyone has approval in God's eyes. We were made just, or righteous, because Jesus paid for our sins on the cross, which means God now sees us *differently*. From His perspective, we are conformed to His own being, His will, and His standard of rightness. We are forgiven and as clean as the purest snow. The decision was already made, and here's the only question: Will we receive this good news or not?

I think the world longs to see they have God's approval and acceptance. He constantly reminds me of His approval—that He does approve of me. "Because we are his children, God has sent the Spirit of his Son into our hearts, prompting us to call out, 'Abba, Father'" (Gal. 4:6).

While I'm worshiping and listening to what God is saying, I often see myself as a small boy, and I'm dancing and playing freely in a field where Jesus sits watching me. "Look at me, Daddy! Look at me!" I say as I spin and twirl in joy before Him. I run into His lap and feel His assurance as He embraces me. Then I run and play again, knowing I have my Daddy's full attention and approval. "Because of Christ and our faith in him, we can now come boldly and confidently into God's presence" (Eph. 3:12). These intimate experiences with my Daddy God are so important in shaping how I see the people around me. If God loves *me* like this, He loves everyone else this way too.

---

1 Strong's Greek #1343.

Even when we're young, a fierce battle takes place within us. We lose the fight when our confidence gets displaced and we feel shame for things we've done or thought. Loneliness and feeling neglected are painful traumas to the human heart. So it is vital we know, without a doubt, that we're cared for, approved of, and completely accepted by the One who created us. We need to set our hearts at rest in His presence whenever our hearts condemn us. The Lord is "greater than our hearts, and He knows everything" (1 John 3:19-20 NIV).

We need a breastplate of righteousness to protect the truth of God's love for us. His body armor of acceptance gives us power to deflect condemnation and rejection. When our hearts begin to judge and condemn the world around us, this is a sign we need to exchange our thoughts for His and allow our minds to rest in His presence. His righteousness changes the way we think about ourselves and overflows into how we see the world around us.

Christ's Ambassadors

Sometimes when I hear news reports about crime, I begin to feel discouraged and distracted—because I've started focusing on the visible signs of greed, hate, and selfish behaviors. In these moments, I need to step back and trust it is the *Holy Spirit's* job to help people see their decisions are harmful.

In John 16:8 Jesus described one of the Spirit's key activities in the world: exposing wrongdoing *and* God's righteousness. "And when he comes, he will convict the world of its sin, and of God's righteousness, and of the coming judgment." Do you see the beauty in that statement? More than pointing out their sin, the Advocate—the Holy Spirit—is also in the business of reminding people about God's righteousness and approval available to them through faith. This is where we can partner with Him and release hope and forgiveness to the people around us. "We are Christ's ambassadors; God is making his appeal through us. We speak for Christ when we plead, 'Come back to God!'" (2 Cor. 5:20). We are not called to convict the world of sin—but to be a beacon of light radiating God's invitation without judgment.

When we start to play God, using our own experiences to decide what is acceptable behavior and what is not, our hearts quickly become unable to bear this weight.

For about a year, I worked at an outreach mission in Santa Cruz where we fed the downtown homeless, clothed them, and shared our faith. It was a great ministry, but as I overextended myself, my heart began to grow tired and hardened toward the people we were trying to help. I began to see them as ungrateful and constantly needy, unable to be satisfied. Recognizing my heart wasn't in a good place, I asked God for help.

A week later I attended a worship conference where I asked God to "create in me a clean heart" (Ps. 51:10). Immediately I felt His presence begin to squeeze my heart—my chest felt like it was being crushed—and I fell to my knees. This experience was like a spiritual surgery, where God healed my heart after it'd become clogged with bitterness.

Until that encounter, I had no idea how much I needed help. I was involved in so many righteous acts, but more than good deeds, God wanted me to carry His compassion so I could represent His unconditional love with sincerity.

We need to protect our hearts because our passion and zeal come from the Spirit of God within us. In Exodus 34:14 when God described Himself, He said His "very name is Jealous" and that He is a God "who is jealous about his relationship with you." The word *jealous* in Hebrew is *zelos*, which means to feel burning love that boils from within.[2] God designed us to be like Him, so it's possible for us to carry His burning love for the world.

> This is what the Lord of Heaven's Armies says: My love for Mount Zion is passionate and strong; I am consumed with passion for Jerusalem!
> Zechariah 8:2

> Jesus saw the huge crowd as he stepped from the boat, and he had compassion on them and healed their sick.
> Matthew 14:14

The word *compassion* in Greek is *splagchnizomai*, which means to be emotionally moved from the inward parts of your body—that is, the seat of your affections.[3] Jesus was an amazing example of how we can see a city and become overwhelmed with empathy for the people who live there.

---

2 Strong's Hebrew #7067.
3 Strong's Greek #4697.

ADVOCATE

God wants us to share in His desire to help other people instead of becoming frustrated and judgmental about their sin.

When our hearts get distracted and become focused on people's faults and mistakes, we end up destroying the hope we're called to carry. When we pray, we can often hear the internal battle going on inside us. We praise God and ask for His blessing over our lives . . . and then in the next breath release annoyance and frustration toward the people He made (Jas. 3:9). He created our voice to bless every single person on the earth and build up everyone with encouragement. Not just believers who know His love, but everyone. I believe God sees every single person with the same passionate love, believer and unbeliever alike, and He chooses to see them forgiven and whole through what Jesus did on the cross. When we put people into categories to separate who deserves our personal kindness and who does not, we're just giving ourselves an excuse to abandon and curse people.

Jesus was talking to an expert in religious law one day, and they both agreed that two commandments—love God and love your neighbor as yourself—are keys to experiencing eternal life.

But the expert wanted to "justify his actions," so he asked Jesus, "Who is my neighbor?" (Luke 10:29). We tend to separate people into groups of "us" and "them," and this helps us feel justified as we show more love to certain people and not to others.

But God doesn't think like that and neither should we. Jesus taught us to forget all political, religious, or moral judgments so we can love anyone and everyone.

Praying for Your City

> You were cleansed from your sins when you obeyed the truth, so now you must show sincere love to each other as brothers and sisters. Love each other deeply with all your heart.
>
> 1 Peter 1:22

If I can "grow" hatred in my heart toward other people, the opposite must also be true—I can grow love that reveals Jesus and changes people's lives.

But how? How can I learn to plant and nurture love in my heart when it feels cold toward others?

Love and mercy will start filling up our hearts as we meditate on the acceptance Jesus has freely shown *us*. The righteousness of God through Jesus cleanses us from sin, but it also has the power to transform the *perspective* of our hearts to love the world as God does, seeing others as family.

Acts of kindness begin with an internal attitude of acceptance and approval toward the people around us. Not acceptance and approval of *sin*, but of the person committing the sin.

Intercession Point

Ask God to overwhelm your logical mind with His compassion for your city. Then from that position of heart, ask Him, "What is the best possible thing I could pray for my city?" Pray as He leads.

Chapter 6

DEFENDING YOUR HEART FROM DISAPPOINTMENT

When I was a new follower of Jesus, I was so full of gratitude and hope that I felt invincible, like nothing could bring me down. God's love mesmerized me, and I knew I had found something real–possibly for the first time in my life.

Fascinated by Jesus, I was shocked when I heard of Christians who suffered from depression and discouragement. *What? Why?* But as disappointments and frustrations slowly began to creep under my skin, they slowly poisoned my heart toward the lost people around me.

If we want to love people the way we're called to, we have to stop focusing on our failures or the failures of the people around us. This is another important part of guarding our hearts.

Jesus was careful to guard His heart from discouraging influences. "The ruler of this world approaches. He has no power over me, but I will do what the Father requires of me"

(John 14:30-31). The enemy can actually gain power over us when we choose to focus on failure or when we allow disappointment and anger to simmer within us. Jesus kept God's passionate love burning within Him by responding to curses with blessing and extinguishing every arrow of accusation thrown at Him.

Through what Jesus has done on the cross, everyone is forgiven and welcomed into God's family, but this truth does not go unchallenged. We all struggle with feeling like we're alone, rejected, and unacceptable. These lies rob us of the ability to see God's heart and how much He wants us to run to Him. He wants to free us from these internal battles and anchor us in His unconditional love.

Defending Our Hearts

Paul used the idea of a shield to describe how we diligently need to defend our hearts.

We use our shield of faith to "extinguish all the flaming arrows of the evil one" (Eph. 6:16 NASB). The word *shield* in Greek is *thyreós*, which basically means a door.[1] A Roman soldier carried a full-body shield made with layers of wood glued together. This was then covered with linen and animal skins and bound with iron. This shield—which was as big as a door—protected soldiers from deadly arrows and gave them greater confidence and courage to move against their enemies.

The devil's "arrows" can come in a variety of packaging.

---
1 Strong's Greek #2375.

ADVOCATE

They can be lies about our identity, any messages that accuse us, and frustrating situations meant to get under our skin and push us into hot-blooded anger and discouragement. These attacks are designed to rob us of our restored identity and the peace we have with God and people. The enemy bombards us continually (Rev. 12:10).

You might not be aware of a voice that constantly tries to speak doubt and discouragement into your heart, but you'd probably recognize the enemy's words. The accuser, as the apostle John called him, tries to prove you're bad and undeserving of heaven's love. Have you ever felt that way—that you're messed up and God would be better off picking someone different? That's the enemy's voice.

All of us have made mistakes and done wrong things, but we're not decisively unredeemable—because of Jesus. The enemy proclaims day and night, "This person is bad!" But God chooses to look past our mistakes and believe in our value and future.

When we fall into criticism and accusing others for their faults, this is the complete opposite of intercession. Jesus welcomed sinners with open arms, and He defended their right to be loved and believed in. He fights for "sinners" even up in heaven: "If anyone does sin, we have an advocate who pleads our case before the Father. He is Jesus Christ" (1 John 2:1).

Many of us are deceived and duped into imitating the prosecutor of the world—instead of learning from the Advocate, who helps and comforts people. Does God believe people should face consequences for their actions? Absolutely. "Don't be misled—you cannot mock the justice of God. You will always harvest what you plant" (Gal. 6:7). But only He can decide if someone is beyond all hope.

We're called to stay clear of judging others and concluding they're unworthy. Too often we partner with discouragement and don't use the shield of faith to fight off accusations and feelings of shame within ourselves; we then spill out this inner pain on other people and become a prosecutor of the world.

Extinguishing Fiery Arrows

Before a battle, Roman soldiers would soak their shields in water so the shields wouldn't go up in flames when the enemy launched "fiery arrows"—arrows dipped in tar and lit on fire.

The Greek word used in Ephesians 6:16 is *sbennumi*, which means to "extinguish" or "quench" these fiery arrows.[2] When you pour a bucket of water over a campfire, you cancel the chance of that fire continuing or of another fire starting anytime soon. That's what the believer's shield of faith does—it effectively shuts down the enemy and accomplishes the opposite of what the enemy planned.

Jesus didn't come to the earth just to *protect* us from the devil—He came to *destroy* what the devil was doing (1 John 3:8). God wants to heal us from the wounds left by

---

2 Strong's Greek #4570.

the arrows launched against us: all the lies, bitterness, and frustrations that undermine who we really are. He wants us healthy and whole, so we can step into our destiny of releasing life and healing to everyone around us.

"We bless those who curse us. We are patient with those who abuse us. We appeal gently when evil things are said about us" (1 Cor. 4:12-13). Faith empowers us to release the opposite of any accusations against us, and we don't have to get caught up in the tangled web of blame.

Just like Jesus did on the earth, we can carry acceptance, love, and mercy deep in our hearts, so we're able to extinguish the flaming arrows meant to destroy us and the people around us.

> If you are a thief, quit stealing. Instead, use your hands for good hard work, and then give generously to others in need.
> Ephesians 4:28

Paul understood we aren't just forgiven for our sins—that isn't where the story ends. Our destiny is to *reverse* our self-centered mindsets. If we allow Him to do so, God can completely transform us so we start to live the opposite of destructive habits and attitudes. This kind of active faith gets people's attention and helps transform the culture around us. When we embrace God's love, power, and hope for our lives, we step into a faith that overcomes our fears.

We've been given an opportunity to step into a momentum that counteracts the enemy's plans and helps us move forward into our God-given destiny. "Don't let evil conquer you, but conquer evil by doing good" (Rom. 12:21). When we activate the shield of faith in our lives, loving our neighbor—and even our enemy—becomes quite possible.

The Issue with Bitterness

> Those who are peacemakers will plant seeds of peace and reap a harvest of righteousness.
>
> James 3:18

In addition to changing our attitude toward people "out there" who are living in sin, we need to learn to extinguish and silence any accusations we're shooting toward family members, friends, or the nation we live in. This is hard—in fact, it isn't possible to do this in our own strength.

I constantly need to submit my thoughts to God and listen carefully for His wisdom, because I've learned I can't effectively pray and intercede for people if my heart is clouded with offenses and anger.

When we receive God's peace in our hearts, we can sow His loving-kindness toward ourselves (which is life changing) and the world (which can be nation changing). It is more important to become a *peacemaker* than just to pray for peace. We need to carry light within us in order for real intercession to take place. Cultivating an atmosphere of faith and hope toward the world is essential, and I've come to think it's more important than just begging God to help us by changing our situations.

The enemy knows if we walk around upset, we will sting others with the same angry toxin. Bitterness spreads like weeds. "Watch out that no poisonous root of bitterness grows up to trouble you, corrupting many" (Heb. 12:15). If there is hatred hidden in our hearts and we don't deal with it, it goes deep into our souls and changes the atmosphere around us. We want to affect the people around us with our blue peace instead of corrupting those around us with red anger.

But again, this is where the shield of faith comes into play. Our faith in God—believing His Word, that He is good, that He is with us, that He loves us, etc.—shields us from the effects of everyday annoyances.

It's similar to how skin works. Like a shield, our skin was designed as a barrier from bacterial infections that could turn into something more serious. The word *bitter* in Greek is *pikros* and means to cut or prick your skin.[3] At first we might not think a little thorn prick can hurt us, but if that small hole isn't dealt with, it can turn into a deadly septic infection. Likewise, anger and resentment quickly neutralize the hope and love God has called us to share with the world.

Jesus used thorns to describe subtle and deceitful things that try to hinder our spiritual maturity (Matt. 13:22). The goal is to let His love bear fruit in our lives and not allow life's stresses to keep us from growing. If we're going to shine hope to the world, we need to learn to extinguish and counteract the little pricks in our skin. The call on

---

3 Strong's Greek #4088.

our lives is too important for us to let painful or unjust circumstances steal away the joy and hope essential for our spiritual health.

The Issue with Anger

> "Don't sin by letting anger control you." Don't let the sun go down while you are still angry, for anger gives a foothold to the devil.
>
> Ephesians 4:26-27

Sometimes when I'm in line at the grocery store, I start to feel the anxiety and stress of the person behind me who's in a hurry. When I'm driving, I can pick up on other people's restlessness and find myself driving more aggressively, like I need to win a race.

Paul warned about the dangers of anger and how much this powerful emotion can influence and manipulate us. The word *foothold* in Greek is *topos* and means to give someone a seat or an opportunity to be with you.[4] When I think about this definition in regard to the enemy, it starts to feel a little creepy. I don't like the thought of taking the devil out for coffee and allowing him to speak into my life, but that's what I'm doing when I let anger get under my skin.

When I'm angry and curse someone, most of the time I can instantly feel my mistake—it's like I'm ingesting poison. Snakes first pierce the target's skin with their fangs and

---

4 Strong's Greek #5117.

then pump venom into the bloodstream. The venom is designed to paralyze the victim, making it that much easier for the snake to devour them. Like a snake's poison, bitterness and anger weaken our outflow of love and hope and make our spiritual lives feeble and ineffective.

Peter, one of the most famous people in the New Testament, once allowed frustration and the need to control to influence him to the point where he spoke the enemy's heart. And instantly regretted it because of what happened next.

> Jesus turned to Peter and said, "Get away from me, Satan! You are a dangerous trap to me. You are seeing things merely from a human point of view, not from God's."
> Matthew 16:23

Our human perspective can seem right and helpful in the moment, but it can distract us from what God is saying. Later in Peter's life, he focused on being filled with the Spirit and listening to God's leading. He transferred his attention from the human perspective to God's perspective, and the results were amazing: "Sick people were brought out into the streets on beds and mats so that Peter's shadow might fall across some of them as he went by" (Acts 5:15). Peter became a vessel for God's presence, and the world was never the same.

God wants to *radically* deliver us from anger's downward spiral and set us free to release healing and blessing toward the cities we live in. "Our lives are a Christ-like fragrance rising up to God" (2 Cor. 2:15). How amazing would it be if we could step into a room and people would immediately recognize the presence of heaven, even before we said a word?

Purposefully Releasing God's Love

When my sister got married, my wife, daughters, and I arrived early because of family pictures. It worked out that I had a lot of free time before guests arrived, so I decided I would walk around and pray quietly in tongues, just to see what would happen.

As I greeted people, I purposefully set my mind and heart to bless every person I saw. I don't really like attending formal events or dressing up, but I decided to put aside my normal complaints and have a good attitude instead. After the event, I learned that one of my sister's friends had felt God's presence when I walked past her, and her cold disappeared. God wants our lives to be so saturated with His presence that we bear fruit greater than the thorns.

When we focus on *only* blessing the people around us, we step into our destiny as ambassadors of God's love. Our true identity has nothing to do with our mistakes. The enemy wants to condemn and distract us from a more important reality—that we can rest in God's love for us. (We'll talk about this more in a later chapter.) The world can be so busy pointing fingers at people that it never stops to see God's open arms and acceptance. We want to be different.

Praying for Your City

Most of the time, it's important for us to go directly to God so we can hear His voice for ourselves. But at other times, we need someone who can help us "see" the truth about who we are and what God is saying. Historically these prophetically gifted individuals were called *seers* (1 Sam. 9:9).[5] God is always speaking truth that brings hope, joy, and peace into our personal lives and situations. If we can't hear His voice for whatever reason (discouragement, fear, hopelessness, etc.), we can find someone else who can. We don't ever need to be afraid of the prophetic voice of God, because it always strengthens, encourages, and comforts us (1 Cor. 14:3).

God's perspective is Jesus. When He sees us, He sees Jesus because our lives are "hidden with Christ in God" (Col. 3:3). Without that revelation, we have a hard time seeing what He sees. Our perspective of the world and ourselves can easily become distorted by the enemy's lies. These lies "blind" us and keep us from seeing things clearly.

God's truth—how He sees us—is reality. The Greek word for "pride" is *typhóō*, which means vision distorted by smoke. Or in other words, having a *hazy* mindset.[6] It's a lie when we believe we're "above" everyone else and don't need to listen to anyone—but it's *also* a lie when we tell ourselves we're worthless. Both mindsets are illusions that fog our vision.

---

5 Strong's Hebrew #7203.
6 Strong's Greek #5187.

God wants our eyes clear and our hearts clean so we can intercede for our cities with hope and expectation.

Intercession Point

> When was the last time you were offended? Pray a blessing over the person involved. Ask God to empower you with the shield of faith so you can extinguish any fiery arrows or temptations for destructive anger shot in your direction.

Chapter 7
BELONGING COMES BEFORE REPENTANCE

One night I got together with some intercessors to pray and intercede for our city. We decided that repenting for the city's sins was a good place to start. It made a lot of sense to me. Repentance is necessary to clear the way for blessings—right?

I was thinking about repentance and blessing when I heard the Lord speak to my spirit: "I bless people before repentance." He added, "You have no idea how much you sin. If you were to see all of it, you would be overwhelmed. I bless you continually—even though you will never repent for every sin."

Well, that little encounter succeeded in changing my perspective. I began to intercede in a new and *lighter* way. Instead of trying to carry the heavy burden that "detailed" repentance can sometimes produce, I just allowed God to lead my prayers. As I did this, it was like my spiritual eyes opened, and I became more aware of the favor and joy God felt toward my city and how He loves to see those who don't know Him yet from this same hope-filled perspective.

Many believers don't pray for their city or nation because they get overwhelmed when they look at all the mistakes people are making. It's similar to the awkwardness and shame parents can feel when their children misbehave. We start thinking we should repent for our children's sins like Job did:

> Job would purify his children. He would get up early in the morning and offer a burnt offering for each of them. For Job said to himself, "Perhaps my children have sinned and have cursed God in their hearts."
>
> Job 1:5

When we focus on a record of wrongs, we can easily be overwhelmed and start to forget about God's forgiveness and plan for our lives. Staring at darkness doesn't help us. When I focus on people's mistakes *more* than I reaffirm my love for those people, I find a reason to separate my heart from them. This perspective creates an unnecessary tension and inevitably results in that relationship becoming strained and distant. If I'm constantly seeing the negative in people, after a while I don't even want to think about them because I'm trying to avoid feeling frustrated and hopeless.

Dwelling on all its sin doesn't encourage me to pray for my city with hope and expectation. Fixating on people's shortcomings does not lead me to hope or a belief that God has a beautiful plan for all of us, our children, and our nation.

God Makes No Distinction

In the early days of the church, certain Jewish believers thought that Gentile believers should abandon their native cultures and restructure their lives to follow strict Jewish laws and customs. But Peter disagreed:

> God knows people's hearts, and he confirmed that he accepts Gentiles by giving them the Holy Spirit, just as he did to us. He made no distinction between us and them, for he cleansed their hearts through faith.
>
> Acts 15:8-9

This attitude needed to be corrected because the Jewish believers were essentially building walls to keep people out. They separated people into two groups—"us and them"—while supposing their own culture was far superior to that of the Gentiles.

Peter, however, had learned that God doesn't separate people. He makes "no distinction."

That's how God thinks about you and me. The word *distinction* in Greek is *diakrínō* and means to discriminate, doubt, separate, and to "over judge" in a negative way.[1] When God sees you, there is no doubt about His

---
[1] Strong's Greek #1252.

overwhelming love for you. He doesn't hesitate for one second. He doesn't stop because your sins have gotten in the way of His love.

God sees a clear path for His kindness to flow into people's lives—despite their failures or "unique" lifestyles. We need to think the same way God does if we're going to truly intercede for our cities.

My family heritage is Native American and Western European. Half of each. Sometimes when people find out I am part Native American, they treat me differently. Some people choose to give me honor, while others have responded with disdain or even jealousy because of my skin tone. Personally, I resent it when someone likes me or dislikes me based on race, color, or heritage.

On the other hand, I love it when people look to see my heart and get to know me without prejudice. National or racial pride can be dangerous when it blinds us to people's hearts. It's so important we learn to see people with a clean slate and have an attitude that allows us to learn from anyone, including those who are different than we are. *Always learning* is what it means to be a disciple. All of us have room to grow. We can learn how to replace our human or worldly ideas with God's truth.

In order to see the gold within a person or nation, we first need to take our focus off their history of successes or mistakes.

Empathy, Not Sympathy

The deepest need in our hearts is to belong. Every child and adult longs to be listened to and seen as valuable.

When people merely *sympathize* with you, they consciously or subconsciously look down on your situation and feel sorry for what happened. Empathy is the better response. It actually tries to imagine what your situation is like and how it feels. Empathy engages your heart so you can truly get to know another person.

When Jesus walked the earth, He didn't look down on people but truly empathized with them. He attracted outspoken sinners to Himself because He sincerely cared about their hearts and carried hope for their restoration. Listening with your heart engaged, and expressing your engagement with your body language, releases healing into people's souls.

> Rejoice with those who rejoice [sharing others' joy], and weep with those who weep [sharing others' grief].
>
> Live in harmony with one another; do not be haughty (snobbish, high-minded, exclusive), but readily adjust yourself to [people, things] and give yourselves to humble tasks.
> Romans 12:15-16 (AMPC)

If we're going to position our hearts to intercede for our cities, we need to adjust our attitudes and actually *identify* with people. We need to allow God to lead us into His perspective, one that embraces people and creates an atmosphere of belonging even before they've repented for their mistakes.

In the same way, when someone is struggling and comes to us for prayer, we need to be sensitive and adjust our footing until we're standing beside them, on their level. Giving advice without empathy is different than encouraging and building someone up. We can't help someone from a distance—we have to draw near with our mind and heart, involving our emotions until we can respond with genuine compassion and concern. As Mary Pytches says, "Our acceptance is not enough. Troubled people also seek our understanding of their plight. It requires an effort to get under the skin of another person, to enter his world, to see and feel it as he sees and feels it."[2]

When I was in elementary school, I found myself in a surprisingly competitive environment. I constantly felt the need to earn my peers' approval so I could stay in the "cool kids' club." In the public schools I attended, fighting was common and I learned to join in, bullying those perceived as weak. My daughters, however, attend Christian private schools, and they've grown up in a different atmosphere. Their schools have worked hard to create safe environments where students can thrive.

---

2 Mary Pytches, *A Healing Fellowship: Guide to Practical Counselling in the Local Church* (London: Hodder & Stoughton Religious, 1988).

One day I decided to attend my daughter's weekly chapel, just to see what it was like. During the service, a boy got up and shared a testimony about how he was bullied in the past. He talked openly about the pain this experience caused him and also shared how God was healing his heart from fear. When he finished speaking, I was shocked as a roar erupted from his peers. The other boys cheered for him and yelled out how awesome he was.

I had never seen anything like that—young boys encouraging each other so freely. When I was their age, the culture I was a part of celebrated making fun of each other and criticizing weakness. We celebrated one another—but we had to earn it. You were celebrated only when you did something cool, when you rebelled, or when you scored points for your team.

But that boy who spoke in my daughter's chapel was loved, accepted, and celebrated just for who he was. His culture empowered him and actively worked to free him from past rejections.

If belonging is one of our most vital needs, how can we meet this need in others' hearts?

Smiling at Your City

A few years ago, I knew my dad was sick and wouldn't have many more years with us. So I asked him to share about his childhood and what he'd learned over the years. To my surprise, he wrote me the following email:

When I was very young, I wondered what I would become. I wondered how I would serve God and earn my way to the final reward of heaven. Should I become a doctor, a minister, or a volunteer in Africa? I was walking down the street one day and passed by a complete stranger. As we passed by each other she smiled at me. Her smile made me feel good, like I had been blessed by an angel. I thought to myself, "That is an example of doing God's work on earth." You may not become someone famous or do something that garners substantial notice, but you can have a positive impact with as little as a smile. Smile at your loved ones. Smile at the children of God. And most importantly, smile at yourself.

Love always, Dad

My dad rarely shared about his beliefs or his thoughts on God, so when he shared this insight with me, I knew it meant a lot to him. I think his description about belonging, accepting yourself, and smiling at others is the good news in action.

Could "smiling" at a city be a key part of God's work on the earth?

Helping people feel loved and accepted is crucial to your being a light within your city. God asks people to trust Him with their whole lives, so it's essential they first understand they are accepted and welcomed just as they are. As my dad suggested, sometimes we get confused about what gives us significance and enough value to enter heaven one day.

Jesus told the crowds in John 6:29, "This is the only work God wants from you: Believe in the one he has sent." God isn't asking you to become something you aren't in order to please Him. He just wants you to relax and believe in His love for you. "Human effort accomplishes nothing" (John 6:63). Our effort doesn't change God's persistent love for us. Many of us have a hard time accepting the gospel because the idea of faith alone goes against our performance mindset. A performance-based mind confuses God's intentions and obscures His heart.

Jesus openly accepted the worst of sinners because He stood in the knowledge and experience of complete approval. "God the Father has given me the seal of his approval" (John 6:27). The word *seal* in Greek is *sphragizó* and means to seal with a signet ring. It signifies ownership that comes with the owner's security and full authority. Similar to how a wedding ring signifies a lifelong commitment, this seal signifies something belonging to someone.[3]

Jesus overflowed with acceptance toward others—because He was secure in the Father's unconditional and unlimited love. He had no belief system that kept Him from embracing the prodigals of His society. So He was

---

[3] Strong's Greek #4972.

able to be friends with and include people like Judas in His inner circle (John 6:70-71). Judas, so it seems, never put his complete trust in Jesus, but Jesus didn't hold this against him. He never separated His love from this man who would one day betray Him.

"Those the Father has given me will come to me, and I will never reject them" (John 6:37). That was and is one of Jesus's core values—that no one in the world is so bad that He'll reject them.

God's arms are always open wide to everyone. He wants us to be His ambassadors and show the people around us that they exist in His heart. So all of us need to grow in *His* attitude, which believes and hopes in people.

Our extravagant Father is watching and waiting for sinners to come home and find out they belong with Him and He accepts them completely. "You are included among those Gentiles who have been called to belong to Jesus Christ" (Rom. 1:6). The word *called* in Greek is *klétos*, which means being invited or summoned by God either to a special office or to salvation.[4] Everyone has a place in God's kingdom, and He is welcoming all to step into their true destiny and purpose.

An amazing plan exists even for those we might consider enemies to the gospel. I know former Satanists and people who used to practice witchcraft who came to believe in Jesus and found their true calling in His family. God eagerly waits for us to bring His love into the world so we can witness that love in action.

---

4 Strong's Greek #2822.

Praying for Your City

For several years now, I've attended Burning Man with a group of believers who carry God's desire to see everyone come to know His love. We sit with people and share the "destiny readings" or encouraging words we feel God leading us to speak. We freely bless people, and God always shows up powerfully. I go to this event each year excited all over again about how much God believes in people.

On one occasion, I sat down with a guy to give him a destiny reading and release hope into his life. When I looked at this man with my natural eyes, I saw a good-looking dancer who was right at home in this environment. I shut my mind off and spent a few moments listening, and God gave me a specific message for this man.[5]

Somewhat hesitantly, I revealed I saw a supernatural gift of writing being imparted to him from heaven. That was all I said, and I was shocked as his eyes filled with tears. My spiritual senses awakened as I felt God's heart for him.

"I'm a professional writer," he told me and shared he'd recently been offered a huge writing contract. "How did you know this about me?"

I explained that his Creator saw him and was always there to help him.

These kinds of experiences are so profound to me. When I surrender my mind to God's heart, I get to experience

---
5 Sharing with people is always a risky adventure, but I've found the rewards outweigh the dangers.

His pride and joy over people. If I believe in the gospel, I should never judge or see that writer out in the desert just as a partier again. I should never see *anyone* the same way again. The Father loves all of us, and He wants to open our eyes to see His truth about ourselves and the world.

For me, encounters like that one reverse and transform my natural mind. Luke describes what happened to the crowd as they watched a paralyzed man stand up in front of them completely healed. "Everyone was gripped with great wonder and awe, and they praised God, exclaiming, 'We have seen amazing things today!'" (Luke 5:26). The Greek word used in this sentence for "wonder" is *ekstasis*, which is where we get the word *ecstasy*. *Ekstasis* is defined as a distraction or disturbance of mind caused by shock or amazement. The root word means to completely remove or take out of a regular position or standing.[6]

That's what our hearts need—a *shock* of love to cleanse them from a performance-oriented, judgmental mindset. Just as a caterpillar transforms and goes through metamorphosis, our minds need to shift and start to see the world differently. We need to meditate on God's amazing love for people in order to reverse and escape the boundaries of our natural minds. "Let God transform you into a new person by changing the way you think" (Rom. 12:2).

When people find out they are called by their Creator and invited to belong to Him, everything can change. We speak God's heart into the world as we show His radical love.

---

6 Strong's Greek #1611.

> For God was in Christ, reconciling the world to himself, no longer counting people's sins against them . . . God is making his appeal through us. We speak for Christ when we plead, "Come back to God!"
>
> 2 Corinthians 5:19-20

My rational mind needs to be displaced so I won't count people's sins against them. I need God's mercy to influence me into a place of amazement, even godly ecstasy, that suspends my normal sensibility. I want to enter a realm where I can see my city from His perspective and ignore or even displace the critical voices within myself, so the one message inside me is a clear reflection of God's heart for my city.

Intercession Point

> Ask God to give you the mind of Christ so you can really start to believe that anything is possible for your city. Meditate on His amazing love and then pray for your city as He directs you.

Chapter 8
LISTENING TO HEAVEN FIRST

One time I was complaining to God about a friend of mine, a person I had allowed to frustrate me to my core. I was by myself and no one could hear me, so I shouted out my grievances.

After my temper tantrum subsided, I hesitantly asked God what *He* thought about this person and their influence in my life. To be honest, I wanted only to confirm with Him that I was completely innocent of any wrongdoing and that the other person was not worthy of my time.

As I calmed down, I closed my eyes so I could focus on God's perspective. In my mind's eye, I saw the person I was so frustrated with coming down from heaven and into my life. They were dressed in white and looked perfect, like they were the best version of who they are.

"I gave this person to you as a gift," God said, and I could feel His heart break. He didn't say these words directly, but it was like He asked me, "Why are you rejecting this beautiful gift I have given to you?"

As I allowed this revelation to penetrate the barrier I had built to keep this person out, it was like my heart began to reawaken. I started to see value in this person and actually felt grateful they were in my life.

After this exchange with God, I hoped the circumstances in my relationship with this person would change, and they did—a small amount. The main thing that became clear was how I needed to mature and develop gratitude and empathy toward other people. It bothered me to realize that in a moment of rage, it seemed I would rather *abandon* a gift from God than learn how to appreciate it.

Part of the good news is that everyone is a perfect gift. Judgments can quickly blind our minds and lead us to reject the people we are called to love and even receive from.

I can't wait for others to change before I choose to love them. I need to be the one who takes responsibility for the absence of love in my life. Jesus highlighted this issue when He said, "You don't love me or each other as you did at first! Look how far you have fallen!" (Rev. 2:4-5). The Greek word used here to describe abandoning God's love is *aphiémi,* which means to send someone away.[1] It's like divorcing your spouse or just giving up on a lifelong friendship. In every lasting relationship, daily forgiveness and mercy are essential. We're called to commit to loving

---

1 Strong's Greek #863.

ADVOCATE

the world—and we aren't allowed simply to *divorce* our hearts from people.

The good news calls us to believe in a higher standard of love. More than once I've heard someone complaining about someone else, and the person listening says, "Just forget them." When we disagree with lifestyles or beliefs, it's easier to push those people to the edge of society rather than deal with our own spiritual immaturity.

I don't think it's wrong to get frustrated with people, especially those who have hurt you. But when our anger demands punishment and wants to erase that person's value—that's when anger becomes transgression.

> You have heard that our ancestors were told, "You must not murder. If you commit murder, you are subject to judgment." But I say, if you are even angry with someone, you are subject to judgment!
>
> Matthew 5:21-22

When people say, "So-and-so can go to hell!" they're basically expressing a desire for that person to be eternally dismissed and labeled forever as a worthless, empty-headed idiot. Believing someone should be cast aside, rejected, and not welcomed back into society is just as serious as committing murder.

We waste energy when we persecute people and point fingers at them. Holding on to accusations against others paralyzes our prayer lives. Instead, we're called to become intercessors who *choose to defend* people and look for God's perspective about individuals or a city. We are called to nurture a joyful expectation that God is moving in *every* person's life—even in the lives of those who are participating in immoral or depraved behaviors.

God wants us to develop an internal atmosphere that openly invites sinners into His family.

Listening to Heaven First

Secure in His identity, Jesus operated from a place of acceptance with His Father that allowed Him to pour out mercy even to the most undeserving person. These extravagant encounters don't fit nicely inside our minds because they challenge our performance-based thinking.

When Jesus was confronted with a married woman who was caught sleeping with a man who was not her husband, the town leaders said to Him, "According to the law of Moses, we should stone her. But what do You say?"

Jesus didn't answer right away. He just stooped down and wrote in the dirt with His finger (see John 8:5-6).

When Jesus crouched down and wrote on the ground, I think He was using this time to focus and listen to what the Father was saying. The beginning of intercession starts with waiting for guidance. Jesus turned away from just reacting to the question—and started listening to what heaven was saying.

ADVOCATE

God often speaks in "a gentle whisper" (1 Kings 19:12). If we want to hear Him, we frequently need to shut out all the distractions.

Too often when people pray for their city, their prayers come out of their own experiences, and they end up trying to *teach* instead of just being a vessel that communicates God's thoughts. Prayers that come from our minds end up being a mix of advice and our own personal desires for our cities. To effectively intercede for cities, we need to prioritize what heaven is saying. Replacing our prayers with living words from God is true intercession.

In this woman's story, the wisdom that came down from heaven literally caused everyone to stop. They dropped their stones of judgment and slowly walked away.

Jesus's answer sounds simple at first, but it carries the weight of heaven: "Let the one who has never sinned throw the first stone" (John 8:7).

As spiritual leaders, we need to cleanse our hearts from prejudice about a city *before* guiding a group in prayer. When we focus our prayers on another's faults, we inadvertently teach the people listening to us to adopt a religious and judgmental mindset. But as we let go of our offenses, we help the people on our teams to drop their stones as well.

None of us have a right to throw stones—even when we're absolutely certain of another person's fault. We've all made mistakes and subsequently need to have mercy for everyone. We should never release divisive prayers that create a saints-and-sinners attitude.

After everyone had gone, Jesus stood up and said to this woman, "Where are your accusers? Didn't any of them condemn you?"

"No, Lord," she replied. (See John 8:10-11.)

When I read Jesus's gentle response to this situation, I think about all the prayers I've prayed that were judgmental and critical. All those internal "comments" I made about what other people should be doing with their lives—those comments were a complete waste of my time. It's like Jesus was saying to this woman, "Where are all those accusations piled up against you? Did any of those 'opinions' reach heaven and influence My Father's opinion of you?"

I don't want to waste my time, energy, and passion on things that are none of my business and end up causing me stress. There are times when I just need to step back and drop the stone of judgment I'm carrying.

We face many confusing situations in our lives that can be extremely difficult to navigate, but God wants us to let Him guide our hearts and minds through every question we have trouble answering. We need to learn to drop our judgmental thoughts and quick answers in order to really hear what He's saying.

For a season in my life, I felt frustrated with everything around me. I kept going to God with my angry questions, and I eagerly waited for Him to fix my problems. One day I took a road trip to get away and spend time soaking in prayer. I began to feel truly peaceful for the first time in a while.

In this place of peace, I heard God say, "You are getting lost in all your questions. Stop asking questions."

Many times my questions aren't good because at their core, they're actually accusations. I say things like, "Why does this person do it that way? That isn't the way I would do it." I'm not trying to understand their thinking—with a critical heart I'm expressing my disgust and anger.

This skewed perspective caused me to fall into a depression where I lost my joy and peace. But once I committed to God to stop asking about other people, my joy returned and healing came to my heart.

Free to Listen to His Voice

The daily onslaught of bad news in the media has caused a lot of confusion, partly because it directs our focus away from loving people to seeing them as problems.

It's easy to judge the world and brand some people as "evil" and some as "good." Many people think the solution to apparent chaos is to point out what they consider to be dangerous and then gather around them others who share the same fears. The problem with this paradigm is that we're called to be consumed with God's love *first* and be led by the One who is slow to anger. Yes, a lifestyle of sin is dangerous because these actions bring pain into the world. If we love the Lord, we need to hate evil (Ps. 97:10). But when we look at the world and see *only* the problems as displayed by the media, we lose hope and neglect to rejoice in the good that surrounds us too. There is always good, because there is always God.

You and I are not anointed to be the guardians of the entire world and carry every burden we read about on social media. Jesus repeatedly spoke to His followers about not worrying or being afraid:

- Don't worry about these things.
- These things dominate the thoughts of unbelievers, but your heavenly Father already knows all your needs.
- Seek the Kingdom of God above all else, and live righteously.
- Don't worry about tomorrow.[2]

Based on those statements alone, I realize I need to be careful with my thoughts and not allow them to become weighed down by heavy circumstances that don't belong to me. God wants our minds to be free to handle our daily problems *with Him* as we listen to His leading. He wants our hearts to be so full of His mercy that we're able to bless anyone He brings across our path. We become living

---

2 See Matthew 6:31-34.

intercession when our hearts are free to listen to His voice instead of being manipulated by worries.

We're called to carry peace and forgiveness into the community where we can make a difference:

> But if your enemy is hungry, feed him; if he is thirsty, give him drink; for by so doing you will heap burning coals upon his head.
>
> Do not let yourself be overcome by evil, but overcome (master) evil with good.
> Romans 12:20-21 (AMPC)

Paul showed us here how we can do our part practically and simply—within our neighborhoods and in the spheres of influence we already have. I am convinced the main thrust of my prayers and concern for others should be focused on the community I live in. God may lay other things on my heart, but no one can take on every world issue they read about.

Go and Sin No More

The way Jesus addressed the woman caught in adultery fills me with hope. Jesus told her, "Neither do I [condemn you]. Go and sin no more" (John 8:11). The word *condemn* in Greek is *katakrinó* and means to judge as worthy of punishment.[3] Jesus didn't look down on this woman but lifted her up and even somehow identified with her—He accepted her, even though she had sinned. His attitude

---

3 Strong's Greek #2632.

provided an atmosphere of assurance and belonging so if she wanted to, she could move forward into a new life.

When He didn't condemn or reject her, this clearly revealed the opposite was true instead. When He said, "Go and sin no more," He acknowledged that her lifestyle needed to change and even implied God would "go" with her to help her turn her life around. Her restoration was His main concern.

Letting others know they have someone they can turn to, no matter what they've done, strengthens them and gives them what they need to move forward. This loving connection with God empowers us to leave our lives of sin and be filled with hope for a good future.

Praying for Your City

Do we have the same attitude as Jesus when we come face to face with people who have decided to live sinful lifestyles?

A few years ago, I was invited to join a group of believers planning to minister at a porn convention in Las Vegas. When I talk about trips like these, many people express some concern about showing grace to those who work in this industry. Obviously, sexual sins distract people from their true calling and destiny, and adult entertainment has powerfully influenced our generation.

But the goal in attending these events is to make connections with porn stars, listen to their stories, and encourage them to see their true value. God wants us to be free to bless *every* person, no matter what they're involved in; He never wants us to curse anyone. No one is helped by an attitude that justifies rejecting others or thinking certain people are hopeless cases.

One day while we were at the convention, my friend struck up a conversation with a porn star at the next booth. Porn conventions are *loud*, so I couldn't hear what they were saying. As I waited in the background, I began to listen to God for an encouraging word that would let this woman begin to see how He knows and loves her. She was working at this event, which means my friend and I didn't have a lot of time to engage her in conversation. So I asked God for one really powerful word she would never forget.

I felt like He told me, "She loves pickles."

I froze. He wanted me to walk up to a porn star and say, "Hey, you love pickles"? I told God, "There is no way I am going to just say this one thing. You have to give me more."

"Her dad loves pickles as well," God replied. "She is like her dad."

Even after getting this additional information, I was still nervous and had no idea what this word meant.

When my friend finished talking with her, I had a brief window in which to share this curious message. I went up to the woman, introduced myself, and asked her if she liked pickles.

To my surprise, she smiled and said, "Yes, I love pickles!"

"Does your dad like pickles?" I asked.

Again with a laugh, she immediately said, "Yes! He loves pickles."

I was on a roll, so I shared, "I feel like God is saying that you're just like your dad."

She immediately burst into tears, covered her face, and ran to the bathroom to clean off the mascara streaming down her cheeks.

When she returned, she excitedly pulled out her phone and showed me a selfie she'd taken three days earlier. In the picture she was sitting in a restaurant and holding up a big pickle spear.

"How did you know I love pickles?" she asked.

I began to explain about how we try to listen to what God is saying about people, so we can encourage them. When I said "prophetic words," her eyes lit up and she knew exactly what I was talking about.

"I grew up going to church," she said. "My dad is a pastor."

She was overwhelmed that we would come to this event and encourage her by letting her know she isn't alone. This word was also a reminder to her that she was running away from her true identity. All of us make this mistake at different times in our lives.

As she and I continued talking, I heard God say to my heart, "This is your sister." Before saying goodbye, I shared that with her and she agreed with a big smile.

God wants everyone to know He will never leave them. When we align our hearts to listen and see from His perspective, it exposes a religious mindset that prevents us from seeing people's true identity. He wants us to reflect His mercy toward every person in our city. We are all alike in many ways, and empathy equips us to shine His light into the world.

Intercession Point

>Ask God to help you see people through His eyes of compassion and mercy. Ask Him to help you love broken people—especially those who aren't repentant or willing to change detrimental behavior. Then from this place of compassion and mercy, pray for your city.

Chapter 9
THE RADICAL AGENDA OF GOD

When I met Jesus, I became an avid fan of worship music. One artist in particular stood out to me because of his style and charisma. His lyrics had a huge influence on me, and his passion helped crystallize my theology about God's goodness and love.

So when I learned he'd confessed to multiple extramarital affairs, I was devastated and the high value I placed on him vanished.

My anger over this worship leader's actions was so strong that I stopped listening to his music. A week earlier, these songs had helped me enter God's presence and were invaluable in developing my intimacy with Jesus. But now it was different. Because of what this man had done.

The harsh realization that this person wasn't perfect shook my faith. Confusion rocked me. But when I asked God about the situation, His response was not what I expected.

"You still read the Psalms and worship through those songs, don't you?" He asked.

I knew exactly what He was saying, and the truth pierced right through all my judgmental standards to reveal my hypocrisy. I read King David's musical psalms every day, and they were a great help in connecting me with God's heart. But I chose not to be distracted by the fact that David had an affair and even committed murder. I was willing to forgive David—but somehow felt I could justify denying forgiveness to someone who was still alive and currently influencing people I knew.

As I considered these things, I could feel God asking me to forgive this worship leader and sing his songs just like I did before. But I wasn't able to. In my mind I'd made the decision to delete and reject this person's music from my life. I felt torn inside and, at the time, it was just easier to forget the issue and not deal with what God asked me to do.

I think a lot of people, myself included, really enjoy God and love the way He loves us. The problem is, when I say I love God but then don't want to personify or express His heart to others, I become a liar and choose to misrepresent His heart (1 John 4:20). In order to become an intercessor, I first need to surrender my whole mind, heart, and soul to God's radical agenda of loving *everyone*. His goal is for His love to be "brought to full expression in us" (1 John 4:12).

A religious agenda wants to be associated only with those who look good in the eyes of the public. If I were running for city office, having dinner with known criminals would be political suicide. But that's essentially what Jesus did. People said, "He's a glutton and a drunkard, and a friend of tax collectors and other sinners!" (Matt. 11:19). Jesus didn't care what religious people thought of Him. His mission was to be love to everyone He met, and the results changed the world. He showed us what it really means to love God as He built friendships with people who didn't share His values.

I didn't want to be associated with or even listen to a worship leader who had sinned like this and hurt so many people. How could I believe this person was still righteous in God's sight?

Even after God corrected me about this, my religious attitude prevented me from looking foolish in the world's eyes. Honestly, I wanted to be identified with outwardly sinless, upstanding believers. As a leader, I was supposed to be an example of purity, right? But in my pursuit of purity, I was willing to kill off anyone I felt made me unclean.

Recently I read about a ministry school leader who was accused of inappropriate behavior and labeled unsafe. I knew many people who were connected with this person, and I felt drawn to find out what was really happening, because then maybe I could help my friends.

A lot of gossip gets through the "fence" because it sneaks in under the guise of wanting to "pray for that person." Personally, I really like gossip. I sincerely appreciate how it makes me feel powerful and self-righteous. "Rumors are dainty morsels that sink deep into one's heart" (Prov. 26:22). All of us are tempted to sign on as jury members in whatever negative, crazy, or painful situation is happening around us, but allowing negative information about people into our hearts doesn't help us become more loving toward the world.

After thinking hard about this topic, I took myself off this particular jury and realized God had never asked me to get involved or even to *think* about this incident. Others were meant to hear this case, and hopefully they helped bring healing to everyone involved.

Too many of us allow bad news or someone else's mistakes to distract us from our true calling. When too many people are involved in a conflict, it intensifies and expands what should be worked out between a select few.

God Is Always for Us

God's point of view is often radically different than ours. Most of the time when we think about the word *judgment*, we picture a person being scrutinized or punished for what they did wrong. When the Bible says, "We must all stand before Christ to be judged" (2 Cor. 5:10), many of us feel a little apprehension because one day we're going to be exposed, and it might not go well for us.

But the truth is, God judges us in order to expose encouraging deeds He can reward. He's looking to see how He can celebrate you. Because of Jesus, we should actually *want* God to judge us.

ADVOCATE

Understanding the truth that God is *always* for us is vital. He is never critical or looking for a reason to punish us. He convicts us of our sins, but it's always for our personal health and benefit. Repentance is a step into wholeness; it is not a headfirst push into discouragement.

At times the presence of the Holy Spirit has deeply convicted me of sins that were causing me pain. One time it felt like God grabbed my heart with His hand. I actually felt the weight of His love compressing my chest. For two days straight, I cried off and on as I felt His jealous love persuade me back into His arms.

> For the kind of sorrow God wants us to experience leads us away from sin and results in salvation. There's no regret for that kind of sorrow. But worldly sorrow, which lacks repentance, results in spiritual death.
> 2 Corinthians 7:10

God is our Advocate, which means He publicly stands by our side, supporting us so we can move forward into an abundant life. The opposite of an advocate is an antagonist or enemy who fights against us. Which of these attitudes do we adopt when we look at the world? Are we full of hope, standing with sinners as their friends? Or are we prosecuting and distancing ourselves from people we disagree with?

Our religious mindsets like to place people in boxes of "naughty" or "nice" so we instantly know how to think about them: approvingly or disapprovingly. But Paul presented a different idea: "Christ's love controls us. Since we believe that Christ died for all, we also believe that we have all died to our old life" (2 Cor. 5:14). My flesh loves to control my little section of the world, and I naturally categorize the people around me so I can make better sense of that world. Allowing God to lead me and letting His love control me do not come without a mental fight on my part—I need to surrender my whole mind, body, and soul in order to live a life that believes the best about people and doesn't judge them by their lifestyles.

Paul gave us a key to living out our faith in the world:

> So we have stopped evaluating others from a human point of view . . . For God was in Christ, reconciling the world to himself, no longer counting people's sins against them.
> 2 Corinthians 5:16, 19

Every time we evaluate others from a performance perspective, we need to repent—some of us may need to repent *a lot* because it's so hard for us to believe all people have value. Our perspective needs to be focused on connection and relationship, not the potential reasons to ignore others.

Paul put on the Father's heart when he expressed joy over others. His perspective focused on the good within them, and he celebrated their value: "After all, what gives us hope and joy, and what will be our proud reward and crown as we stand before our Lord Jesus when he returns? It is you!" (1 Thess. 2:19).

ADVOCATE

Every person in the world has the same longing for acceptance and recognition within their hearts. "Look at me, Daddy! Look at me!" At their core, people desperately want the Father to celebrate who they are and what they've achieved. We need to know we're valuable and making a difference in the world—we need our heavenly Father's smile of approval.

We get to focus on people's good deeds and let them know God sees the beauty within their actions (see Rev. 22:12). We have the ability to create a welcoming atmosphere that encourages them to enter God's presence. I don't think we need to be awkward about it and stand on the street corner, yelling, "The Spirit and the bride say, 'Come!'" But we can nurture an open mind that welcomes the Spirit of God to come into every area of our lives. We are called to carry God's presence to people who are thirsty—and invite them to encounter the One who loves them.

God Sees the Good

God wants every person to know He sees the good within them. When we realize how He looks at us—not to kill us but to reward us—His love breaks down walls and our intense fears of rejection.

In Acts 4:10 when the angel appeared to Cornelius, the man was terrified:

> Cornelius stared at him in terror. "What is it, sir?" he asked the angel.

> And the angel replied, "Your prayers and gifts to the poor have been received by God as an offering!"

It seems that Cornelius, like most people, was scared of what God thought about him. He saw the angel, and his first response was terror. In deep encounters with God, people often feel vulnerable because He can see every good or bad detail of their lives.

But this angel didn't focus on Cornelius's sin or all the mistakes he'd made during his life. Instead, the angel focused on the good in Cornelius's life and this judgment—that Cornelius had done well—opened up the man's heart to receive the good news.

If God "receives" our prayers and gifts as offerings, He must notice and celebrate even the smallest acts of kindness.

When Paul entered Athens, his heart turned toward the people, and he felt burdened to share the hope and truth of Jesus. He explained to them:

> His purpose was for the nations to seek after God and perhaps feel their way toward him and find him—though he is not far from any one of us. For in him we live and move and exist. As some of your own poets have said, "We are his offspring."
> Acts 17:27-28

Paul wasn't fixated on the city's sin. He didn't proclaim, "Your great sin is keeping the Lord at a distance! And if you don't get this fixed, you're in danger of hell!" No, he chose to look at God's heart for this city and how His presence is *close* and available to everyone. He even quoted one of their poets and acknowledged the good already within their culture. Paul saw every one of these people through the lens of hope and the faith that they would soon be connected with the God who loved them.

When I first started listening to God, I felt Him impress on my heart that I should cut my hair. I had dreadlocks at the time, a style I associated with my identity as a drug dealer.[1]

The next "major" change God spoke to my heart was to get rid of my music collection. That one was difficult for me, because music was a major passion and influence in my life. I had a big collection of classic rock from Jimi Hendrix and The Who, as well as some valuable first-edition bootleg recordings of the Grateful Dead playing live. I loved this stuff, but I knew what God had told me, so I began to replace my beloved collection with Christian rock and worship.

Though eventually I grew my hair back, for over twenty years I listened only to Christian music. For a long time, I held a rigid religious view that non-Christian music would lead me away from God. I felt like it celebrated sexuality, drugs, and the mystical spirituality that had left me empty before Jesus. By rejecting secular music, I felt I could lift myself above the culture around me.

But one day—twenty years later—I woke up with the song

---

[1] Technically, I don't believe having long hair is "wrong" for men, but God wanted to get rid of an attachment and identity in my life.

"Just Like Heaven" by The Cure running through my mind. All day long I couldn't get that song out of my head, so I looked it up on my phone and played it in my car several times in a row. The song is pretty catchy, but I felt like it didn't have much meaning or depth. I sat there and argued with myself about why I would spend my day listening to a band that had once released an album titled *Pornography*.

Frustrated, I asked God, "Why can I not get this song out of my head?"

"I am singing this song to you right now," He replied.

Immediately my heart swamped with the sensation of His pursuing love chasing me down. The lyrics came alive as I felt God speak His love directly to me. My religious mind told me this kind of music would *keep* me from God—but He was using this song to open my heart even wider to His love.

That is just one of many experiences I've had with secular music, art, dance, teachings, and films. God speaks through many different expressions, and understanding this has helped me see the good within the people around me, even those who are actively running away from Him.

Paul was so interested in the Roman culture that he could quote their poets. When we honor and look for the positive things within different cultures, we open our hearts toward the people God made in His image. Getting to know the world's creativity and culture equips us to see the beauty within people.

Praying for Your City

One night at the Burning Man festival, I was out late listening to a DJ who was playing deep trance music. Within the music were overlays of a mystical teacher speaking about how we are all spiritual beings. The music was amazing, and all I could see was how hungry people were for true spirituality. It was like I could feel the desire of their hearts to know God and be known by Him.

In the shadows nearby, I noticed a man sitting on a bike. I felt like God said to me, "He is a man of God."

Though I felt a little awkward, I stepped closer to this guy and asked if I could share a revelation with him.

"Sure! Go ahead," he said, seeming completely open.

So I told him what I'd heard. He looked right into my eyes and exclaimed, "Yes, I am. Do you have any more words to share with me?"

As I began to sense the journey he was on, I described it to him, and he shared with me some deep questions that were heavy on his heart. We ended up laughing in joy together, and he gave me the longest brotherly hug I've ever received.

I've learned that as I look for the good within other cultures, a doorway of hope swings wide inside me. Today I am much more open to giving and receiving love from God in any shape or form He chooses.

If we spend our time focused on people's faults and judging them based on what *we* think they should be doing with their lives, we are not adding anything positive to the situation. We're just trying to play God.

> I told you not to associate with people [in the church] who indulge in sexual sin. But I wasn't talking about unbelievers who indulge in sexual sin, or are greedy, or cheat people, or worship idols. You would have to leave this world to avoid people like that . . . It isn't my responsibility to judge outsiders.
> 1 Corinthians 5:9-10, 12

We aren't called to *leave* the world and avoid people. The opposite is actually true. With an empowering and *inviting* mindset, we get to engage the world. Paul made it very clear that judging those outside our sphere of influence is none of our business. God has given us an opportunity simply to rest in His love and have hope for all people. Focusing on sin and judging life choices isn't helpful when it comes to bringing love to the world. Instead, we get to change cities with *hope*.

Intercession Point

> Ask God to help you see how you can engage people in your city this week. Pray for your city, believing He welcomes every person into relationship with Him.

Chapter 10
HOW YOUR EXPECTATIONS CAN CHANGE YOUR CITY

At Burning Man each year, more than fifty thousand people come together to build a sprawling camp out in the desert. The event is considered an "experiment" of living in community. Artist-dreamers and engineer-administrators work together to help this temporary makeshift community function successfully.

While I was deciding whether or not to attend this event for the first time, several of my friends expressed concerns about the possible dangers of this kind of "free culture." I think some of these concerns were valid, but I wanted to focus on God's perspective and learn more about how to love people. All people. Even the weird ones. So I went anyway.

One morning during the event, I was worshiping God and listening for His voice when I saw a picture of milk and honey pouring down the "street" where we were camping. This vision encouraged me to believe God was already pouring out His goodness into people's lives. My team and I decided to go meet people and just bless them.

To my surprise, every person we met was very open to our love and wanted to connect with us. We had an open door to release God's compassion and healing over *many* people in a short time.

When we reached the end of the street, I turned around to look out at the *massive* number of people camping in the desert. At that moment, God spoke very clearly to my heart. "Look, the fields are white for harvest!" I could feel incredible hope and excitement inside me as I looked at this nomadic city, and I *knew* my heart was feeling what God felt. This experience was a game changer in how I view cities and how I believe God wants us to see the world.

It's time for us to retire our faithless fears so we can pick up the Lord's hope and expectation *for more*.

Most of us have a basic understanding of what it's like to grow something. Maintaining a healthy, fruitful garden takes a lot of work! We have to break up the soil, sow seeds, pull weeds, water the plants, and deal with insects before we get the reward of a harvest. Those are the foundational "rules" of gardening.

Yet when it comes to people and what He's doing on the earth, God doesn't always follow the rules we're used to. Jesus taught His disciples a supernatural way of thinking about planting and harvesting:

ADVOCATE

> The Lord now chose seventy-two other disciples and sent them ahead in pairs to all the towns and places he planned to visit. These were his instructions to them: "The harvest is great, but the workers are few. So pray to the Lord who is in charge of the harvest; ask him to send more workers into his fields."
>
> Luke 10:1-2

Some of us need to change our minds about evangelism and how we can impact our cities—it doesn't have to be hard. The harvest is "great," which implies it is ready *right now*. It is waiting *right now*. Many of us look at our cities and say, "Oh, it isn't time yet. It will be wonderful and amazing when God moves here, but He isn't moving here right now."

Jesus gave His disciples a brand-new perspective on reaching people: "But I say, wake up and look around. The fields are already ripe for harvest" (John 4:35).

The time has come for us to stop looking at the world with traditional expectations. When we look at the world with natural eyes, we can easily get overwhelmed with all the work that needs to be done. But Jesus wants to resurrect our hope and change our perspective until we start to see the world as ready to receive His love—right now. When He looked at the "fields," He could see a huge revival happening, and that is what He wants us to see as well—that our cities are ready *today*. Imagine what it would be like for thousands of people in your city to receive Jesus and be filled with real peace for the first time in their lives. Imagine a supernatural harvest where everyone was full of joy and celebration because of the truth of Jesus!

Historically, harvest time in Israel was a season of great joy and satisfaction that lasted for about seven weeks. During this time, workers brought in grain, grapes, and olives, and pilgrims would migrate from surrounding areas to help. Gathering the harvest is hard work—but it is much more satisfying and rewarding than planting and weeding. When we start to feel like transforming cities is difficult and labor intensive, it's a sign our perspective needs to change. Jesus declared it's harvest time!

The world is ready to respond positively to Jesus. We need to carry a hope within us that believes the harvest is ripe and abundant. When our primary source is God's perspective, anywhere can look ready for harvest!

Looking Through Spiritual Eyes

Abraham was a spiritual leader because he chose to trust God's promise that he and his wife would have a child in their old age. From a human standpoint, such a thing was impossible, but God had plans:

> God told him, "I have made you the father of many nations." This happened because Abraham believed in the God who brings the dead back to life and who creates new things out of nothing.

ADVOCATE

> Even when there was no reason for hope,
> Abraham kept hoping.
> Romans 4:17-18

In the natural, Sarah was ninety years old—obviously well past the age of childbirth. But Abraham kept hoping, even when there were no signs his hope would come to pass.

Similarly, we have no reason for hope when we look at our cities with natural eyes, but like Abraham, we are called to see with *spiritual eyes*. We get to look into a realm the natural world does not acknowledge and rejoice in our hope.

It's time for us to see the world as forgiven and pure because of Jesus. No matter how "bad" or lost people are, there is still the hope they will receive His forgiveness and come into relationship with Him. *Right now,* they are completely ready and acceptable in God's sight. He's already dealt with their crap—they just need to come.

The world's main issue is they don't believe Jesus died for their sins (John 16:9). Most people are painfully aware they've made mistakes, but the truth that God loves them and has already forgiven them seems too good to believe.

> Oh, what joy for those
> whose disobedience is forgiven,
> whose sins are put out of sight.
> Yes, what joy for those
> whose record the Lord has cleared of sin.
> Romans 4:7-8

When I choose to delete every record of offense from my mind, I can feel the glory of God. When we see the world in this light—when we choose to overlook the sin to reach the heart—we become able to pray for entire nations with passion and expectation. God has already done the heavy work on the cross, and it is now time to see people through hope and joy. We can make the daily choice to remove fault from our memory, looking at the people around us with love instead of according to their failures.

The more I see the world from God's perspective, the more encouraged I am to pray and release blessing everywhere I go. I don't like myself when I get critical, frustrated, and quick to judge every situation around me. God's love for people will never stop, but my attitude can dam up my love toward the world. I'm a much better person when my heart is full of love toward the people around me.

Frustrated prayers that focus on another person's faults aren't very effective. When we position our hearts to see people either as deserving or undeserving, we turn ourselves into self-righteous judges. When I'm free from judgment *before* I begin to pray for others, I can tap into God's heart for them much more easily.

This concept is similar to what Paul wrote about giving. The Lord loves a cheerful giver, and consequently I think it's good for us to decide in our hearts how much we're going to give in advance (see 2 Cor. 9:7). Have you decided in your heart how much blessing you're going to give? We don't have to feel obligated or pressured to pray for the world, but when we've decided how much we're going to give, that measure gets to flow freely from the forgiveness we have personally received from God.

I feel deep peace and joy when I spend time positioning myself under God's mercy *first*, before I pray. When I'm focused on His mercy, I really enjoy seeking His perspective about people. It's like I get an insider's view of how He sees that person.

Praying for Your City

Recently I heard some discouraging news about a friend who's struggling with a drug addiction. I hated the thought of how this man was slowly destroying his life.

But one day while I was worshiping and singing, God gave me a picture of this person. I saw my friend in complete health and working as a teacher. He was reading books in a classroom, and all the kids adored him and looked up to him. There was a crown on his head, and his life gleamed with purpose, meaning, and depth. Everything was different.

To me, this picture represents what most people would want for those they love: blessing, good health, a life that prospers. God has a great plan for each of us, even if we have yet to see the workings of that plan. *That* is how I want to see my friend—and how I want to pray for him. This picture gave me hope for this man, and now I can pray with expectation in my heart to see God's vision come to pass.

Seeing my friend this way didn't change his situation, but it did change me. Now my mind is filled with hope and is no longer discouraged. I can believe in this person because I see a future that is full of purpose and redemption. I also believe my attitude has become more attractive and welcoming to this friend, instead of being critical and distant.

If we want to release peace into others' lives, we first have to carry peace ourselves (Luke 10:5-6). You and I are not called to *save* the world but to *love* it. If we aren't secure within God's acceptance, we can develop a mentality where we're the heroes with all the answers, which isn't what it means to show Jesus to people. Introducing others to a life of faith can happen only through love and patience.

> Live wisely among those who are not believers, and make the most of every opportunity. Let your conversation be gracious and attractive so that you will have the right response for everyone.
> Colossians 4:5-6

Our attitudes become more gracious and attractive to the world when we stop *striving and working* for a harvest. If we see the world as valuable, we will naturally have the right response toward the people around us. Unbelievers find generous and pure love attractive—they're drawn to it because it looks like the One who made them.

People are cautious about who they trust. Most won't accept us if we have an attitude that says, "You won't be acceptable to me until I change you. First I need to dig out all those weeds in your thinking and make you give up all your evil ways. Maybe then you'll be good enough to be with me."

On the other hand, when we step into people's lives to bring hope and not correction, interacting with them in humility and vulnerability, they will be more likely to receive us and the love we're called to represent.

It's common for Jewish people to greet one another with the Hebrew word *shalom*. "Peace be with you." This is much more than just a hello. The Jewish blessing of peace involves a heartfelt desire to see the other person completely healthy and happy. Shalom is a declaration of safety, prosperity, salvation, and goodwill.

People can tell if you want the best for them, and peace is inviting and contagious. When we follow 1 Thessalonians 5:16-17 and are constantly joyful and always praying, we become a *living prayer* for our city because we're releasing *shalom* everywhere we go. We can truly declare the blessing of peace if we step into God's perspective that wants everyone to be whole and free.

The peace and rest we carry give people an opportunity to see Jesus. When we look at our city and see the people as Jesus sees them, we will want to build them up. We will see the best in them. We will begin to understand how God is constantly pouring out His kindness over them in hope that they will see how good He is. He'll empower our hearts with His overwhelming love for others. When we have this attitude of love and peace, people will open their homes and welcome God's message of hope.

The harvest is now. All around you, people *long* for an encounter with the living God who believes in them.

Intercession Point

> Spend time with the people in your city. Don't be afraid of those who aren't like you and who might live radically different lifestyles. Practice seeing these people with God's eyes. He deeply loves them.

Chapter 11

BECOMING A TRUE FRIEND OF YOUR CITY

Years ago I befriended an older woman who suffered from severe chronic pain and spent most of her days in bed. For five years I visited her weekly, spending my days off with her and helping her with chores. She had a New Age mindset, and most of her friends called themselves "white witches." She wasn't open to hearing about my faith in Jesus, but she always appreciated my prayers and companionship.

At the time, I was confident in my skills as a pastor and believed she would eventually put her trust in God. She saw sign after sign of God's existence and love for her. When I prayed for her for healing, she often felt peace and experienced temporary relief from her pain. I also tried to share the good news with her in "practical" ways: I cleaned her dishes, organized her closet, took her out to eat, and listened to all her life stories—twice.

But after visiting her nearly every week for seven years, I grew tired and wanted to see some results. Was I or was I not fixing the problem of unbelief?

I had good intentions, but my attitude toward her slowly became bitter because I wanted to see someone transformed who did not want to change. Every time I went to visit this lady, deep in my heart I struggled with a spirit of performance. In the back of my mind, I expected *results*. My attitude was, "Come on! I have been Jesus in the flesh for you. I have shown you His love! Why won't you receive it? Why do you keep resisting?"

Frustrated, I asked God about this, and I felt like He told me, "Even though she may never come to know Me, are you still going to be her friend?" He immediately addressed my agenda and how it didn't align with His.

"Of course, Lord," I replied, sensing what He was asking me to do. "I can do that. I can be her friend."

To this day, the words He spoke still go deep into my heart. He convicted me about how I had seen this woman like a problem I could fix. I repented from my performance mentality and could see that "just being her friend" was the answer. Up until that point, somewhere in my thoughts I'd believed that being someone's friend, and only their friend, wasn't good enough. But I laid down my ambition and pride and instead put on love. "Above all, clothe yourselves with love, which binds us all together in perfect harmony. And let the peace that comes from Christ rule in your hearts" (Col. 3:14-15).

After I repented for my arrogant attitude, my heart shifted. The heavy weight of striving dropped off of me, and I no longer carried a burden or responsibility to see this lady get saved. I wasn't giving up on her, but if she never came to receive Jesus, I was going to be her friend to the end. *That* was a race I could win. I could love her, hold her hand, listen, laugh with her, and comfort her. As my heart changed, I knew God wanted me to be free just to love this woman—and love myself without a performance mindset.

A couple of years later, my friend passed away, and I was with her until the last day. As I thought back over the past year, God said to me, "You could not have done any more or any less for her."

The Holy Spirit speaks into every heart with empathy because He's close enough to our situations to understand what we need. My personality type gravitates toward problem solving. I like to fix things that are broken, and I find it difficult to *stop* working on a problem until I know the solution. This can be a great gift, but relationally it can also be a big problem. People are not machines that can be tinkered with and then yelled at when they don't work properly. You and I aren't responsible to fix the world.

Truly Set Free

Recently during worship, I saw a picture in my mind's eye of Jesus leading me into a wide-open space. We stood in a flat, immense desert where I could see for miles under a crystal-clear sky. A huge sense of freedom pumped through me, and all my worries vanished from my mind.

"Christ has truly set us free," Paul wrote in Galatians 5:1. "Now make sure that you stay free, and don't get tied up again in slavery to the law." When I take the time to listen, God continually reminds me to let go of my worrying thoughts. I get so used to the feeling of striving and trying to perform that I forget how unhelpful and dangerous this mindset can be. Jesus released us from the burdens of the law so we can become living prayers—men and women of God who are so free in Him that we naturally lead people to Him without worry or force or pressure on our parts. I've found I need to be aware of this freedom and maintain it by resisting the temptation to get entangled in situations God has not called me to.

The call to pray for others is *not* a call to take on their problems and clutter our minds with issues that don't belong to us. A few months ago, I watched a documentary about reducing your possessions in order to live a minimalist lifestyle. The goal is to be free of clutter, so you can focus on what is truly important in your life and pursue what brings you lasting happiness and peace. I feel like God is calling me to be a "spiritual minimalist." That is, a person who is focused only on what He's calling me to. I don't have room to worry about anything else.

In Luke 12 someone tried to pull Jesus into their personal business:

> Then someone called from the crowd, "Teacher, please tell my brother to divide our father's estate with me."
>
> Jesus replied, "Friend, who made me a judge over you to decide such things as that?"
>
> Luke 12:13-14

ADVOCATE

If even *Jesus* had to guard Himself from getting involved in another person's affairs, so do we! After this conversation, He shared a story that illustrated how we can get distracted by possessions, and He concluded with this statement: "Yes, a person is a fool to store up earthly wealth but not have a rich relationship with God" (v. 21). Many of us strive to fix other people's problems and keep a record of their accomplishments, just like a "fool" would store up earthly riches. Deciding what's good and bad in other people's lives and stepping in as their judge can make us feel powerful, but it distracts us from true relationship with them—and with God too. When our minds are caught up in the world's problems, we end up overstimulated and stressed. A better goal is to be at rest, rooted in God's love, so we can discover our true passions and pursue the unique destiny He made for us.

All of us have different needs, and these needs shift and change at different times in our lives. Some days God wants us to know He's standing by our side, and other days He warns us to stop a behavior that's hurting us. Some days He wants us to learn an important lesson, and other days He just wants us to enjoy His presence as we have fun with Him.

Personally, I think God interacts with every person in the world the same way whether they believe in Him or not. The Holy Spirit shows the world kindness, heals their hearts, speaks peace, and provides for their needs. The same Spirit also gives the world an inescapable awareness and conviction of the sin of unbelief (John 16:8). God constantly, patiently interacts with people to help them experience His love, with the hope that they will eventually trust in His salvation.

I want my prayers to be aligned with the God who is helping, comforting, and standing close to an individual or city. Jesus described the Holy Spirit with the Greek word *paraklétos,* which can be translated to mean helper, comforter, advocate, intercessor, counselor, or strengthener.[1] "But in fact, it is best for you that I go away, because if I don't, the Advocate won't come. If I do go away, then I will send him to you" (John 16:7).

A deeper definition of a legal advocate is someone who takes a stand with you and for you. They're able to make the right judgment call because they know your heart and are close to your situation. Only God is truly able to judge our lives, so without His insight and love, we should steer away from judging anyone else, including ourselves.

Our intercession for a city should always begin from this point:

1. Knowing we are completely forgiven ourselves,
2. Forgiving the city we're praying for, and
3. Listening to God's leading about how we should pray.

If we're going to pray for people, we need to come into alignment with the Spirit who is strengthening them. God stands with everyone as a Comforter and Advocate, and we need to align our hearts with His so we can be *for* people and speak up for them in a holy and godly way.

---

[1] Strong's Greek #3875.

The good news could be described this way: that the courts are closed, and we have been given a full pardon from every mistake. This doesn't mean we don't need to repent, but Jesus paid for everything and it is truly "finished," just like He said. A performance mindset has a difficult time believing it doesn't need to do anything more.

Paul asked, "Who then will condemn us? No one—for Christ Jesus died for us and was raised to life for us, and he is sitting in the place of honor at God's right hand, pleading for us" (Rom. 8:34). Jesus stands with the world and prays for every person from a holy perspective. He isn't like a Santa Claus song, making a naughty or nice list. Instead, He is all about reconnecting our hearts with His so we will be able to see ourselves like He sees us. "He did this to present her to himself as a glorious church without a spot or wrinkle or any other blemish. Instead, she will be holy and without fault" (Eph. 5:27).

When we see the world as accepted and forgiven, as we comprehend that Jesus is in love with the people around us, we can relax and become their friends. Our role is not to judge but to love. How can we love people if our minds are cluttered with their mistakes and problems? God is not disappointed with the world, so our prayers should not emerge from our own disenchantment.

Praying for Your City

When I first came to believe in Jesus, I started a salvation prayer list for every family member, past friend, and recent acquaintance. My list quickly grew so long that I moved it onto a big piece of poster board and hung it on my wall. Whenever I took the bus to my college campus, I would look around at the passengers sitting with me, and my heart would break to the point where I actually started crying, feeling helpless to reach so many with the gospel.

One night I attended a large rock-n-roll concert in an outdoor stadium. In the middle of the concert, I looked at the huge crowd—more than twenty thousand people—and knew how lost they were without God's direction. That was my perspective. In the moment, I felt like I wanted to see them get saved more than God did.

"What about them, Lord?" I asked, feeling desperate.

I'm not sure if I saw a vision or if I actually went somewhere, but immediately I was in the presence of Jesus.

I looked to my left and saw walls made of clear stones that sparkled from within. Men with beards stood lined up before Jesus with scrolls in their hands. Jesus Himself wore a white robe, and light poured out from Him and shone all around His body. This light was brighter than the sun, but I wanted to look right at it.

Jesus extended His arms to me and looked at me with the most loving eyes that pierced and overwhelmed my heart. The look on His face answered all my questions—I knew He loved the world more than I could possibly imagine. His arms were open wide to them, and He wanted me to rest, knowing He was in love with them too, just as He was with me.

When this scene ended, I cried so hard it felt like sprinklers were going off in my eyes. A huge weight had been lifted from me. I still prayed for people everywhere I went—but now I understood God's love was in control and His heart for the world was much greater than mine ever could be.

Intercession Point

> Every morning for the next week, get up and spend a few minutes reminding yourself of who you are in God. Ask Him to help you remain in His love and believe you're fully accepted in His sight. Then practice *allowing* this peace to overflow into the culture around you (Luke 10:5-6).

Chapter 12
THE GOOD NEWS OF REST

Several years ago, I worked full time as an associate pastor. My wife and I had two small children, and I spent my one day off each week visiting two elderly ladies who were bedbound and isolated. I was exhausted and starting to get grumpy. (At this point in the book, perhaps that doesn't surprise you.)

For a couple of weeks in a row, I didn't make it over to visit these ladies, which was rare for me, and I started to feel like I really needed to go visit them. I went to see one of them in the morning, thinking this would leave me enough time to get some much-needed chores done at my house. However, cutting short a visit with a desperately lonely person is pretty much impossible, so three hours later, I was driving home with my to-do list shooting flames at my head.

I always visited both ladies on the same day, but this time I just didn't think it would work. My big plan was to try to forget about the second lady and get home to do the things I needed to do around the house. As I was thinking through this plan, the second lady called me.

"Where have you been?" she asked anxiously. "Are you coming to visit me today?"

Hesitantly I told her I'd visited the other lady and didn't have time to visit her as well.

She then shamelessly guilt-tripped me for not coming to see her and let me know just how deeply she would love a visit. I had been visiting these ladies consistently for the past five years and was tired. My life was filled up. I was *busy*, and somewhere along the way I'd burned out and grown frustrated.

Again I explained, "I have too many chores to catch up on, and I just can't make it over for a visit today."

I finally got off the phone, but instead of feeling relieved, I felt torn up. In the privacy of my car, I yelled to God, "Why do I not want to do this anymore? What happened? I do not want to visit anyone else today." I could feel something was "off" in my heart, but I didn't know what it was. I used to want to serve these two women, and when I loved them by going to their homes and being with them, I felt like I was loving Jesus. But my zeal had gone up in smoke.

I felt God say, "You do not believe the good news."

"What?" I replied. "I'm a pastor. I *preach* Your good news! I know Your Word. What are You talking about?"

ADVOCATE

I know this might sound arrogant, but that's often how I talk to God. I let Him know what I'm feeling and when I don't understand something. It's a bit "untraditional," I suppose, but I'm confident my confusion doesn't hurt His feelings and that He doesn't mind my questions.

Again I heard, "You don't believe My good news."

Once more I had a little tantrum because now I was starting to wonder if maybe I didn't know what I was doing—according to God, I didn't even know the basics!

Finally, feeling rather humbled, I asked, "What do You mean? What is the good news?"

Immediately the Spirit's presence flooded my heart. He said, "If you were to do nothing more to serve Me, and you sat on your couch the rest of your life and only took care of your wife and kids, I am going to be so glad and pleased to see you when you enter heaven."

These weren't just words appearing in my mind; I *felt* them as they rose up and overwhelmed my spirit. It was like these words had physical weight, and God took them and pressed them into my heart. I could feel His pleasure and acceptance all over me. He was ecstatic with joy over me. I started weeping and had to be careful because I was trying to drive. So much undeserved grace.

"Lord, I don't believe this," I said in repentance and awe. "Help me to believe Your good news."

I could see clearly, in black and white, how I'd been striving to earn His approval. It was not enough for me just to receive His work on the cross. I felt I had to *do* something to earn my acceptance. My message was "works" and not good news at all.

The real good news is so far beyond my understanding, my pride, and my ambition. There were times when I'd believed and experienced it, but somewhere along the way, I'd lost the true good news and started believing a lie.

I asked for forgiveness and then tried to imagine doing absolutely *nothing* for God. I pictured myself sitting on my couch for the rest of my life and then being welcomed into heaven afterward with great joy and honor. I began to laugh at the sheer contradiction of my thinking and what I knew now in my spirit. Total acceptance and joy from God roared inside me, but my mind could not make logical sense of it.

As I tried to grasp what God was showing me, I said, "I don't have to do anything more. I don't have to ever visit these ladies again."

Hearing those words out loud moved me to tears. When I thought about these ladies, I felt a surge of energy come back into my spirit—not because I *had* to do something, but because I knew I didn't have to do anything, which made me want to do *something*. Doing good was no longer a burden, a requirement I had to meet. I began realizing that being able to help people was a blessing and an opportunity. Even if I did nothing, I already had my

Father's complete acceptance, honor, and joy—because of my faith in what Jesus did for me.

As this revelation slid into my heart, I wanted to visit the second lady—I even looked forward to it. I called her back and told her my chores could wait a little longer. My to-do list suddenly seemed miles away from what was important because visiting this lonely woman would mean the world to her. She would be so grateful, and how could I pass up the opportunity?

That day, finally, I started to believe the good news—that there are no requirements. I am just as pleasing to God sitting on my couch as when I'm feeding the poor, taking care of others, giving my time, etc. This propelled me into a deeper level of freedom than I had ever experienced.

To this day, I still battle an internal desire to earn my acceptance. I'm never *required* to intercede for my city, but just thinking about the good news of Jesus inspires me to intercede because discovering God's heart for people is fun and rewarding. The "gospel of the couch" has become a launching point for me to persevere in prayer and continue learning to love the world. Jesus wants our giving, in whatever form it comes, to spring from generosity and not obligation.

The Gospel of the Couch

Rest is difficult when our eyes are focused on all the problems around us. The key is to realize the battle is over and step into the rest of God:

> So there is a special rest still waiting for the people of God. For all who have entered into God's rest have rested from their labors, just as God did after creating the world. So let us do our best to enter that rest. But if we disobey God, as the people of Israel did, we will fall.
>
> Hebrews 4:9-11

What does sitting on the couch make you think of?

I start thinking about relaxing with my family, watching a movie, laughing with friends, putting my feet up, reflecting on the good things God has given me. To me, the couch represents peace from every battle and enjoying life and my acceptance in God's embrace. On God's couch, I can receive what my Father is saying to me. "Well done, my good and faithful servant. You have been faithful in handling this small amount, so now I will give you many more responsibilities. Let's celebrate together!" (Matt. 25:23). When I understand how God accepts *me,* I am empowered to lead more people into His rest.

On the couch, the good news digs deep roots within my heart. When I get bothered and stressed out with life's problems, I can't hear or see the truth of the good news. I quickly become blinded by my own self-determination to fix the world.

My intercession needs to come out of my time on the couch, where my perspective is full of hope and light. Jesus told Paul, "Yes, I am sending you to the Gentiles to open their eyes, so they may turn from darkness to light and from the power of Satan to God" (Acts 26:17-18). When my eyes are focused on darkness and the power of Satan, I begin to slip and fall. My heart grows weary and bitter when I'm consumed with problems. But when the eyes of my heart repent and turn toward the light, everything changes. That's when I have hope for *stadiums* of people—I see whole cities coming to know Jesus. I see wave after wave of revival sweeping across the land. My heart begins to burn with expectation and looks to see what God is doing around me.

Repentance is not a one-time act but an ongoing lifestyle of exchange. On the couch, I turn from works and learn to see from God's perspective. When I'm at rest in His acceptance of me, I can listen to people with empathy and not anxiously throw out answers to their problems.

I am convinced the couch is the answer for the world. All of us need to know about this special place where we can commune with our Father. To be living examples for the world to see and follow, we need to become *excellent* at rest and peace. The world wants to enter a place of acceptance and joy with God, but it needs people to show it the way. I need to receive God's rest if I'm going to believe and pray for others to enter His rest with me.

In order to release the flow of God's presence everywhere we go, the key is to experience His love. His love is our identity, the foundation that enables us to pray with confidence:

> I pray that your hearts will be flooded with light so that you can understand the confident hope he has given to those he called.
>
> Ephesians 1:18

> Then Christ will make his home in your hearts as you trust in him. Your roots will grow down into God's love and keep you strong.
>
> Ephesians 3:17

> May you experience the love of Christ, though it is too great to understand fully. Then you will be made complete with all the fullness of life and power that comes from God.
>
> Ephesians 3:19

As we're *grounded* in God's love, we will naturally want everyone around us to experience His love as well. Spending a lot of time on the couch can seem like a waste when there's so much to be done, but that thought is actually a lie. In this place of rest, our roots mature and absorb all God's love for us—and for the world around us. Our hearts need to be flooded and overwhelmed with light in order for us to carry hope into the world.

When I know I don't *have* to pray in order to please God, I am free to pray from my heart. I get to partner with Him and release His healing that empowers other people with hope. On the couch, I can have a flowing conversation with Him all day long, and there I realize I've been given an opportunity to change the world around me. Praying for my city is a reward I am invited into—and it is a great honor.

Praying for Your City

When I was courting Cecilia, I spent a month in her home country of Sweden getting to know her culture and the city where she lived. While she was at work, I wandered around visiting tourist sites and praying for people. I would often get words of knowledge for strangers, and I enjoyed sharing these encouraging messages with them. I love to hear God's voice, and my ongoing conversation with Him frequently spills out into other people's lives as well.

One day when she and I were visiting her church, God gave me a specific word of knowledge for the pastor and the church. It's one thing to give words to people unrelated to her, but speaking to her pastor was an entirely different story. I did not want to share this word because it felt out of place for me to do so. I wasn't a member of this church, and I didn't even live in this country. How was it appropriate for me to speak into the leaders' lives?

I never shared the word, and the next day I felt a shift in my conversation with God. Something was different. I felt Him tell me that for the next two weeks, I wouldn't get any words of knowledge for anyone.

I didn't understand. Yes, I knew giving that word to the pastor was important, and I had blown it. But why was I being disciplined for it?

For the next two weeks, I listened for God's voice for other people and nothing came. Frustration crept in, and I started to feel like I was starving because I couldn't hear His voice like I had before. But in this time of quiet, He showed me something. I realized how much I love hearing His heart for people. This wasn't an obligation for me—it was a gift, an amazing reward in my life. In the end, I was so thankful He took it away so I could see what a joy it is. When I don't *have* to do something, I then get to do it for the right reason, because it comes from my heart and not from obligation. Gifts are a blessing to use, experience, and share with others because we're stepping into our purpose and destiny.

The Father is calling us to become like Him in a deeper way. As we enter His rest, the motivation of our hearts aligns with the motivation of His heart, and we become true advocates for the people around us.

Intercession Point

> Spend time with God resting in His acceptance and unconditional love for you. Ask Him to show you any areas where you feel "required" to perform for Him, and then ask Him why you think that way. Afterward pray for your city—out of a pure desire for others to come to know Him as well.

Chapter 13

FROM ACCUSER TO ADVOCATE

I have two amazing daughters, and I've always been actively involved in their lives. Through the years I've tried to balance boundaries and keep my kids safe—with freedom, so they can make their own choices and develop into mature adults.

When my older daughter was accepted into the college of her choice, I was proud of her, but my joy over her success turned out to be temporary because I started to realize what this acceptance meant.

Anxiety slapped me across the face as I imagined her leaving home and facing adult responsibilities for the first time. One day my uncertainty took over, and I started lecturing her about all the weaknesses I saw in her daily routine. I basically told her, "If you don't correct all the shortcomings I see *before* you move out, you aren't going to succeed in college."

I didn't realize this at the time, of course, but I was envisioning her failure and essentially telling her she wasn't enough. I told myself this was love and that she needed me to give her a wake-up call so she could win. Our conversation was tense, as you can probably imagine, and afterward my chest felt tight and I didn't want to talk to anyone. All I could think about was how she wasn't ready to deal with life on her own and that my obviously loving warnings were being ignored.

My wife was struggling with the same worries and fears. Our daughter was moving out—was she ready for the real world? On our way to church one morning, Cecilia and I discussed all the potential "problem points" we felt needed to be addressed.

But something about the conversation sat heavily on me. I could sense our mindset wasn't right, and I said quietly to Cecilia, "It's time to exchange our thoughts for God's thoughts."

During worship, I asked God what *He* thought about the situation, and He quickly addressed the root issue: "Stop trying to control. You need to step back and watch as she fails."

In my mind's eye, I saw my daughter walking down a path. She stumbled but then regained her balance and kept going. The scene repeated itself a couple of times.

As I let God's words sink in, it was like heavy chains broke off me. I began to realize my daughter didn't need me to judge her competence and help her avoid potential failures—she needed me to support and love her without forcing her to suffer through my know-it-all attitude. I want to be welcomed in her life, and I could see that my controlling attitude would eventually cause our relationship to disintegrate and prevent us from being connected. This corrective word renewed my heart. It freed me from control and instilled within me a confident trust that God has a plan for my daughter. He's a loving Father and the ultimate Friend; He will never leave us, not even when we fail.

After showing me this picture of my daughter walking down the path, God asked, "Do you want to see what you looked like at her age?"

I hesitantly agreed, and a similar picture appeared in my mind's eye, this time of me on the path. I saw myself trip—but unlike my daughter, I fell flat on my face. I completely biffed it, but I picked myself up and kept going.

I started laughing, marveling at God's sense of humor as He busted my critical attitude. Years earlier when *I* had moved out to attend college, I ended up quitting after the first year, so this picture made perfect sense to me. At that age, I was so full of pride that it took multiple headlong falls before I humbled myself and asked for help. Thankfully, God never gave up on me, and I eventually got sober, picked myself up, and returned to college.

Failures are unavoidable on any journey. When we watch someone fail, it means we're accepting the reality that we all make mistakes and we're trusting this person will pick themselves up and grow. All the great champions have what is called a "short memory," meaning they quickly forget their failures and keep pursuing their goals.

God as a Friend

A true friend is there to support and love you even through your failures. God watches us fail continually—and yet He chooses to stick by our side. In the same way, we have the opportunity to follow His lead and walk in patient love with the world around us, without being critical.

Valuing relationship with others is more important than being right. This should be our mindset: "So now we can rejoice in our wonderful new relationship with God because our Lord Jesus Christ has made us friends of God" (Rom. 5:11). Just as God loves us unconditionally and embraces us as His friends, we get to embrace every person in the world as a friend—including those who, in our opinion, "are doing it wrong."

True friendship with people who think differently, who eat weird things, and who behave strangely can only happen when we decide to lay down our critical attitudes. "Stop deceiving yourselves. If you think you are wise by this world's standards, you need to become a fool to be truly wise" (1 Cor. 3:18). Truly wise people learn to lay down their human understanding so they can love those who are different than they are.

Jesus asked, "If you love only those who love you, why should you get credit for that?" (Luke 6:32). God is calling us to love people who do not love our way of thinking. That is, *they* think *we're* wrong. Everyone sees things in unique and different ways, and truly understanding one another is rare and difficult. There is no such thing as "common" sense because everybody's sense is different!

Honestly, if God wants to be *my* friend, He wants to be *everyone's* friend. He wants all of us to feel a deep sense of belonging and be able to trust His heart and dedication. If we can see people as belonging to God even *before* they accept His friendship, our whole attitude will change toward the world.

When my wife was a teenager, her sister invited her to a church youth group meeting. The people in the group made her feel so loved and accepted that she continued to attend even when her sister stopped going. Cecilia felt a sense of belonging she'd never experienced, and it kept her going back. After six months of being a part of this church community, she privately gave her heart to Jesus. There was no pressure to make this commitment, and she was welcomed and accepted no matter what decision she eventually made.

When the Bible says we "exist" in God's heart, it uses the Greek word *eimi*, which means to exist and to *be* purely.[1] It has a timeless implication similar to when God said, "I was, I am, and I always will be." Paul wrote, "But by the grace (the unmerited favor and blessing) of God I am what I am" (1 Cor. 15:10 AMPC).

---

1 Strong's Greek #1510.

My judgmental mind occasionally wants to erase people who have hurt me. I've even said in anger, "Go to hell!" But I have to repent every time I start thinking that way because I'm basically saying, "I don't care if you die. I never want to interact with you again." How could I even think that way? It's the complete opposite of God's heart. Thankfully, He does not execute these very *human* wishes of mine.

What if we reversed that kind of hateful thinking? The opposite might look like inviting everyone we're angry with into the Father's loving embrace. Perhaps we wouldn't say those words aloud, but that would be our heart attitude. We all long to hear, "Welcome home!" from people who love us and genuinely want us around. I believe God wants us to view everyone as worthy of belonging and to recognize they exist eternally in His heart.

Belonging needs to be experienced individually—that is, every person needs to know His acceptance on their own. But God can reveal His heart for people even before they have seen or accepted it. When we allow Him to show us how much He loves and accepts the people around us, we can then help *them* see their calling and destiny.

Throughout the Bible, the people of God had to learn to expect the impossible with Him. He's the One "who brings the dead back to life and who creates new things out of nothing" (Rom. 4:17). We are called to carry hope for people, even when they have no expectation of acceptance. People who don't believe their existence matters could not be more wrong. They do belong, and we need to be the first to believe this for them. God sees everyone in the world as potential friends, so why shouldn't we do the same?

Love Without Conditions

> "I have never eaten anything that our Jewish laws have declared impure and unclean."
>
> But the voice spoke again: "Do not call something unclean if God has made it clean."
>
> Acts 10:14-15

I'm surprised sometimes at how stubborn I am when it comes to learning that writing people off is wrong. But even after spending three years with Jesus, Peter still struggled with this concept, so I suppose I'm in good company.

In Acts 10 when God gave Peter the vision of the sheet filled with animals, Peter's response is typical of a religious mindset that wants to prove its value before listening to God's heart. When we don't understand the love God has for us and how much we belong in His heart, we constantly try to prove our worth.

Peter took issue with the vision's key point: that God has made Himself accessible to everyone through what Jesus did on the cross. Peter was raised with a traditional separatist mindset that didn't allow Jews (God's people) to associate with Greek "pagans" who worshiped other gods. Jews believed that visiting a non-Jewish residence would make them unclean in God's sight. Imagine what it would be like if you were raised with that kind of judgmental mindset and genuinely believed such an attitude was righteous! Changing your mind and learning to think a new way would be really hard. When we believe we are superior to another people and isolate ourselves to "maintain our righteousness," we don't yet understand the gospel.

God wants to destroy any walls separating us from the world, so we can freely open our hearts and our homes to people who are seeking Him.

> Peter told them, "You know it is against our laws for a Jewish man to enter a Gentile home like this or to associate with you. But God has shown me that I should no longer think of anyone as impure or unclean."
>
> Acts 10:28

The word translated "associate" is the Greek word *kola*, which means to join like glue to someone else and become lifelong friends.[2] God is inviting us to go on an adventure with Him and connect with the very people we once expected to "corrupt" us. Anyone can become a friend—if we have an open mind and an attitude that believes condition-less love is a true representation of God's heart.

Jesus cultivated a mindset that invited people to come and meet the Father. He obviously got frustrated with people and situations, but He forgave those involved so quickly

---

[2] Strong's Greek #2853.

that He created a welcoming atmosphere everywhere He went. The world recognized the Father's heart within Jesus and was attracted to His accepting love.

In Luke 23:34 when Jesus said, "Father, forgive them, for they don't know what they are doing," this was more than just a request in the moment—it was an expression of His ongoing attitude. Whenever He saw people doing stupid things or acting foolishly, He quickly let them off the hook because they didn't realize what they were doing.

His phrase "They don't know" uses the Greek word *eido*, which means to appreciate what's happening.[3] It's similar to when people say, "Oh, I see what you mean." *Eido* means perceiving something with your mind and seeing spiritual truth. Jesus carried a merciful attitude because He knew most people wouldn't see how their behaviors affected others.

If I'm honest (and I like to think I am), my human discernment about people and situations can be way off. In general, it's pretty unreliable. I like to imagine I would make a great detective because I can see clues others have missed, but I'm just fooling myself. I really understand what Paul was talking about in 1 Corinthians 13:12: "All that I know now is partial and incomplete, but then I will know everything completely, just as God now knows me completely." All of us are limited in our understanding, and we can't fully appreciate our own behaviors, let alone the behaviors of everyone around us.

---

3 Strong's Greek #1492.

Stephen the revivalist had a similar revelation, and it changed his attitude about the people who wanted him dead. He saw the goodness and kindness of God and recognized that those around him did not—because they had stones in their hands and wanted to kill him. As they stoned him to death, Stephen even prayed, "Lord, don't charge them with this sin!" (Acts 7:55-60).

How could he ask such a thing? They were killing him! But spending time gazing into heaven changes your heart and releases an atmosphere around you that *attracts* those who are spiritually hungry.

What if we carried a heaven-focused mindset into our homes and workplaces? How would this perspective change the way we prayed for our cities?

One of the people present at Stephen's execution was a man named Saul, who later became the apostle Paul, one of the greatest heroes of our faith. But the day of Stephen's death, Saul was one of the "bad guys." Did he see Stephen's forgiving attitude that day, and was it the door that opened his heart to seeing Jesus just two chapters later?

Praying for Your City

After living in Northern California for five years, Cecilia and I felt like God was telling us it was time to move on. My teenage daughter did *not* like the idea of moving away from her friends, and our relationship with her just blew up. She went through a season of intense anger toward us.

I begged God to help her. "Please help her to just survive this move and transition!"

But He immediately corrected my heart. "She is not going to just survive. No! She is going to *thrive*!" He then began to show me how bright her future was and how she was going to end up loving the move and making great friends.

And that's what happened. A year after our move, my daughter could see the change herself—she was sincerely thriving. In fact, she was so glad we'd moved and came to see how God has good plans for her.

God always sees our lives with hope, even when such things seem impossible and our natural minds don't have a clue how good could come out of a particular situation. When the presence of God fills our thoughts, the way we see the future dramatically changes.

"When the Spirit of truth comes, He will guide you into all truth . . . He will tell you about the future" (John 16:13). The *presence of God* leads us into His truth for our lives. In other words, He sees us walking into the great plans He has for us; He sees the masterpiece of our lives and wants to share these encouraging visions with us.

Paul put it like this:

> For we are His workmanship [His own master work, a work of art], created in Christ Jesus [reborn from above—spiritually transformed, renewed, ready to be used]

> for good works, which God prepared [for us] beforehand [taking paths which He set], so that we would walk in them [living the good life which He prearranged and made ready for us].
>
> Ephesians 2:10 (AMP)

God sees your life like a beautiful poem He arranged specifically for you to live out. In the middle of the world's confusion, He wants to help you see everything clearly, from this place of love and acceptance. You can learn to see others through His eyes of truth, and you can help them learn to see clearly too.

All of us have a deep desire to be understood and known by someone close to us. We all want a real friend who chooses us and sticks closer than a brother (Prov. 18:24). As we seek after God and talk with Him, we begin to understand how He knows us better than we know ourselves. This realization is empowering and can liberate us from insecurities and self-doubt. *Belonging* helps us to release hope into our cities and believe God has a plan for everyone.

Since I've had so much practice with judging others, I can tell you a sure key for learning *not* to judge: Spend time receiving Jesus's love for yourself and ask Him to help you see the world through His eyes.

God wants to teach everyone to love themselves *more*, which naturally causes us to love the world more. Empathy enables us to feel a deep understanding toward others. The end goal of empathy, therefore, is to be non-judgmental. How much we stereotype people is a good measure of our relational maturity.

The Spirit of God is opening our eyes to see people without prejudice, and we're learning to feel with our hearts. In this place of amazing freedom, we get to connect with others more effectively and bless them joyfully—because now, at last, we understand. We've realized the great affection of God for them.

Intercession Point

> Ask God to help you see how anyone can become a friend. Believe He has a plan for everyone in your city, and pray that people would come to see His great hope for them.

Chapter 14
WHY WRITING PEOPLE OFF DOESN'T WORK

An inclusive attitude is a must if we want to represent the gospel of Jesus accurately to the world.

For nearly fifty years, Mother Teresa poured her heart into the city of Calcutta. She became "good news" to some of the world's most desperate, hurting people and boldly declared, "If you judge people, you have no time to love them." Her love and intercession for each individual not only transformed her city but caught the attention of the entire world, inspiring thousands upon thousands of people to value those who are often abandoned.

Jesus gave you the same potential to radically change the world. The Spirit empowers *you*—not just others who have more experience—with gifts of generosity, service, prophetic insight, and healing. The world legitimately, genuinely needs *you*.

But it needs you with love. The gifts of God mean nothing to the world without love, and judgmental and critical attitudes can tie up and even shut down the *momentum* of His love. To love people sincerely, we need to be willing to lay down the score pad.

I love my daughters more than anything in the world, but sometimes I can allow my frustration with their growth to overshadow what my heart believes about them. Recently God convicted my heart about this and told me to stop being so critical; instead, He wanted me to listen to His voice about them.

I asked my girls to sit in front of me as I listened to God's heart for them. I wrote down what I saw and heard and then shared these encouraging words with them. All three of us were moved to tears as we felt God's loving presence.

Seeing God's truth will always restore your soul. If I had continued focusing on my daughters' faults, one day I would have found myself an irrelevant part of their lives. When we don't allow the truth of the gospel to set us free from *others'* mistakes, we gradually grow hard-hearted toward our calling to love and stop seeing the good in people.

The good news needs to stay good!

Condemnation Is Catchy

When Jesus said not to judge—more specifically, not to condemn people—He was talking about creating an environment where criticism cannot thrive. A dismissive attitude promotes an atmosphere that is contagious.

When we condemn others, we empower everyone else to do the same, and eventually we will be judged in a similar manner. "Can one blind person lead another? Won't they both fall into a ditch?" (Luke 6:39).

But the opposite is also true. If we continually choose to forgive, we create an atmosphere where people will be encouraged to *grow through* their mistakes. A person's faults can be overshadowed and healed in a culture that emphasizes vulnerability. When judgment is resisted, everyone gets to enjoy a healthy atmosphere where love multiplies. The forgiving culture contained in the Gospels empowers people to be connected and *does not* enable them to continue making toxic lifestyle choices.

Have you ever felt love from a "Samaritan"—someone you might have looked down upon because of their choices or lifestyle? When Paul arrived in the region of Galatia, he was so ill that he needed other people to take care of him:

> But even though my condition tempted you to reject me, you did not despise me or turn me away. No, you took me in and cared for me as though I were an angel from God or even Christ Jesus himself.
> Galatians 4:14

Most Jewish people saw Galatians as "pagan sinners" who were unclean, but Paul was baffled by their generosity as they expressed God's love to him. While he was sick, he experienced what undeserved and unconditional love felt like. He obviously learned from them because he wrote in the same chapter, "Become like me, for I became like you" (Gal. 4:12 NIV).

Only through humility can we see the best in people and recognize the godly characteristics within them. I don't think Paul "became" like them just so he could try to win them for Jesus—I think it was more than that. He embraced their inclusive attitude and could see how God was speaking to him through their acts of compassion. Maybe he even recognized a spiritual wisdom he himself was lacking. Paul doesn't seem like a guy who had a lot of heartfelt connections with people—at least not in the beginning. A judgmental spirit doesn't value people who don't measure up to its standard (Phil. 3:5-7). After meeting Jesus, he probably had to learn how to be compassionate.

What if God led Paul specifically to Gentiles and non-religious people in order to shape his beliefs about how the gospel should be presented? Every people group has different ways they express love and connect with each other, and we can learn something new from each of their strengths. People who say they have no spiritual understanding often can understand love *better* than anyone else and share it with others. Those who readily say they don't have all the answers can be so refreshing to be around.

Over the years, Paul built a great connection with the Galatian people, so much so that the apostle Peter visited these churches and freely enjoyed fellowship with them as family (Gal. 2:12).

ADVOCATE

But then something happened. A legalistic, judgmental group of people traveled from Jerusalem to visit the Christian communities in Galatia. Paul referred to this group as false teachers; they spread a divisive doctrine stating that non-Jewish believers had to be circumcised and follow Jewish rules in order to be received as true Christians. Peter himself somehow got swept up in their religious attitude:

> But afterward, when some friends of James came, Peter wouldn't eat with the Gentiles anymore. He was afraid of criticism from these people who insisted on the necessity of circumcision.
> Galatians 2:12

As this story reveals, a judgmental attitude separates people into categories of worthy or unworthy. This "us and them" mentality is the opposite of the gospel message. When we begin to see people with doubt instead of faith, we are using a performance-based standard instead of believing that God has hope for everyone.

Judgment is attractive, and it's easy to believe the lie that one group is more "superior" than others. We all have an inner desire to be part of an exclusive group that sets us apart, so a little bit of judgment can spread quickly. The other Jews joined Peter in this hypocrisy, "so that by their hypocrisy even Barnabas was led astray" (Gal. 2:13 NIV).

When Paul saw this *unraveling* of the unity they'd once enjoyed, he called Peter out in front of everyone:

> When I saw that they were not following the truth of the gospel message, I said to Peter in front of all the others, "Since you, a Jew by birth, have discarded the Jewish laws and are living like a Gentile, why are you now trying to make these Gentiles follow the Jewish traditions?"
>
> Galatians 2:14

What does it mean to represent the truth of the gospel message? God's heart is filled with inviting love—not a religious fervor that first picks you apart and examines you to see if you've followed all the rules. Can you imagine how disrespected and abandoned you would feel if someone refused to eat with you just because you didn't follow a rule they thought was important? This kind of behavior doesn't reveal what heaven really looks like.

It was a huge statement when Peter chose to separate himself from the Gentiles. Because of his position in the early church, this action had the power to push everyone else to conform and become like the superior "in crowd"—or be rejected and ostracized.

When Paul rebuked Peter the way he did, he wasn't just standing up to Peter, nor was he merely defending the Gentile believers and trying to shield them from pain and rejection. Paul was standing against the judgmental attitude that contradicts the truth of the gospel. Peter was an amazing man of God, but in this situation, his attitude was completely wrong. His actions challenged the gospel message and the lifestyle of Jesus.

When we embrace the idea of loving and accepting those who think differently than we do, we are empowered to become good news to the world. Building relationships with *everyone,* not just those who live and act the way we do, is what Paul called "acting in line with the truth of the gospel" (Gal. 2:14 NIV).

Praying for Your City

In the United States, most people take time off from work to celebrate Thanksgiving and Christmas with family and friends over a big meal. Many of us do this in hopes of creating a special atmosphere where people can make memories and reconnect with each other. These seasonal activities typically interrupt daily life, but that's okay—because we're trying to refocus on something that's more important than work: meaningful relationships.

In the Old Testament, God designed seasons of feasting to build lasting emotional bonds among His people. Eating and playing together are at the heart of every healthy culture. When we sit and enjoy a meal together, it's easier and more natural to overlook our differences, even to forgive. The very act of sitting around a table with others solidifies belonging and acceptance. Feasting together in harmony is essentially the gospel message in action.

The good news compels us to become friends with all people and create a culture where everyone is invited to the table. We're designed in such a way that we thrive as we celebrate God's love and feast together in a spirit of unity. All of us are in need of His forgiveness, and we sit at His table with humility, knowing we did nothing to earn that seat or position.

Walking in the truth of the gospel actually empowers us to sit down at *any* table with anyone in the world—especially those tables where people are throwing out different opinions, motivations, or lifestyles. Eating and laughing with those who are stuck in a self-destructive lifestyle does not "enable" them, like some of us believe. Instead, this kind of love empowers their identity as people who are worthy of a relationship with God.

When people feel a sense of belonging and acceptance, it enhances every aspect of their lives and leads them *away* from behavioral problems. In other words, when we join hands in unity, the people who don't yet understand that God loves them walk away empowered to step up as better and transformed people.

In my journey, it has taken years of praying and listening to God's heart for me to catch His vision for the world. When we truly believe the good news, we become increasingly compassionate and more open to every tribe and every nation in the world.

Inviting others to sit with you and be your honored guests speaks volumes.

> A man prepared a great feast and sent out many invitations. When the banquet was ready, he sent his servant to tell the guests, "Come, the banquet is ready!"
> Luke 14:16-17

That is the essence of the good news coming alive in our world. Letting go of judgment releases freedom to our cities and opens our eyes to see people with hope.

Intercession Point

> Which people group in your city do you "avoid" the most? Spend some time praying for them today, and ask God to show you His heart for them.

Chapter 15
SEEING THROUGH THE EYES OF MERCY

One day something was bothering me, so I stepped away for a little while by myself to refocus my troubled heart. I began to thank God for the good things in my life. Thankfulness is one of the key reasons I worship Him—because I know He's worthy of my gratitude. When I worship Him and am thankful, I come away as a better person. My mind is transformed, my heart softens, my purpose becomes clear, and I feel like I'm being restored to my original intent.

This particular day, I felt like I wanted to move beyond just thanking God for my current circumstances and what He's given me to really show off my knowledge by praising Him for His eternal qualities.

I started by singing out, "You are holy . . ."

But then in my heart, I heard God sing back to me, "*You are holy.*"

My mind could not receive what I was hearing, and I started to argue. "I am not holy—only You are, God!"

So now the singing battle was on. I sang out, "You are worthy . . ." and I heard God respond, "*You* are worthy." I tried to think of more complex words. "You are majestic!"

And God repeated it right back to me, as if goading me to give it another shot. "You are majestic!"

I tried again and again to think of something that could only describe God. He is powerful, everlasting, full of mercy and compassion. Every time I sang a description to Him, He would use the same word to describe me. I finally gave up, still unable to comprehend how God could credit *me* with these attributes.

It took a while for me to start to understand that I am truly holy because of what Jesus did for me. He adores me *like that*. My mind continually needs to adjust out of a performance mindset to see from God's perspective. He's the only One who has the right to judge us. And honestly, if *I* am holy because of what Jesus did—if He adores even me—then He loves everyone the same.

God chooses to see everyone through eyes of mercy, and I need to accept that truth if I'm going to intercede for the world. He thinks differently than I do, so it's vital I exchange my thoughts for His so I can represent His love to my city.

Mercy Is More Important Than Law

Before Paul was known as an apostle and faithful follower of Jesus, he was a strong enemy of the church. We talked about this in an earlier chapter, but here I want to highlight a different part of his story.

Most people see Paul as a crucial example of repentance and God's ability to renew *anyone*. That's very true, but we tend to overlook an important "side character" who played an incredible role in Paul's first days as a follower of Jesus—someone who had to overcome a religious mindset and all his judgmental fears in order to reach out to Paul. This man had to reevaluate everything he believed so he could cooperate with God's perspective.

A Jewish man from Damascus, Ananias was godly, "deeply devoted to the law, and well regarded" by his fellow Jews (Acts 22:12). When someone is "deeply devoted to the law," this usually means they love rules and work hard to perform well. When I'm striving to do a good job and I notice the people around me aren't keeping up, I often get annoyed and, if my attitude continues to go unchecked, I grow resentful toward those I would judge as lazy. People who observe laws are valued by society . . . but a strict adherence to the laws doesn't always mean they're a person who knows how to represent God's *mercy*.

Paul probably terrified a fellow like Ananias. Paul spoke "threats with every breath and was eager to kill the Lord's followers" (Acts 9:1). He had the zeal, power, and authority to fulfill his mission of death, and he was on his way to Damascus, where Ananias lived. All the believers in Damascus had probably heard about this very legitimate threat—but they likely did *not* hear the second part: how Jesus encountered Paul on the road. I imagine Ananias had to stop multiple times throughout the day to surrender his anxieties and fears to God.

Then an unexpected thing occurred:

> Now there was a believer in Damascus named Ananias. The Lord spoke to him in a vision, calling, "Ananias!"
>
> "Yes, Lord!" he replied.
>
> The Lord said, "Go over to Straight Street, to the house of Judas. When you get there, ask for a man from Tarsus named Saul. He is praying to me right now."
>
> Acts 9:10-11

Immediately Ananias started protesting. Paul was a religious terrorist, and all the believers in town likely were in hiding because of him.

> "But Lord," exclaimed Ananias, "I've heard many people talk about the terrible things this man has done to the believers in Jerusalem!"
>
> Acts 9:13

ADVOCATE

What Ananias did was true intercession. He presented his situation to God and waited for a response. He didn't just plead his case, but he *listened* and tried to understand God's heart.

Peter wrote, "Give all your worries and cares to God, for he cares about you" (1 Pet. 5:7). The Greek word *worries* is *merimna,* which means to be divided or fractured.[1] That's what mental troubles do to us—they have the power to divide us and make us weak. God wants us to be whole and restored in His peace. In order to stay calm in a crisis, we need to learn to exchange our thinking with God's thoughts. He wants to overwhelm our fears with His vision of hope, so we will have something to give and not just be paralyzed.

Ananias presented his logical fears and concerns about Paul to God:

> But the Lord said, "Go, for Saul is my chosen instrument to take my message to the Gentiles and to kings, as well as to the people of Israel."
>
> Acts 9:15

We don't know how long Ananias meditated on what God said to him, but it seems like it didn't take long for him to completely reverse his mindset and head out to go find Paul. I imagine Ananias took his first step fearfully, but as he accepted what God was doing, I like to think an incredible peace overwhelmed his heart and mind. As

---
[1] Strong's Greek #3308.

Ananias surrendered his fears and judgments to God, he began to be filled with empathy and courage.

That's the beautiful exchange of intercession. We give God our fears and judgments, and He gives us His peace and courage.

By the time Ananias found Paul, something had radically changed in his heart. We know this because of what he said when he saw Paul. Did he call him a murderous enemy—what Paul had been up until that point? No, he called him his brother: "He laid his hands on him and said, 'Brother Saul'" (Acts 9:17).

How did Ananias go from being afraid of this man to laying hands on him and embracing him as a brother? God never ordered Ananias to accept Paul as family, but Ananias chose to throw himself into God's heart and plans, even if it cost him something. If *Jesus* loved Paul as a brother, then Ananias could too. The empathy in Ananias's heart could grow *only* as he surrendered his critical judgments about Paul and accepted him as God saw him. This intercession or exchange within his heart allowed God to transform Ananias so completely that he became a living example of God's love on earth. Ananias became love to the most unlovable person in his world and began to see his environment through the filter of divine hope.

If Ananias could see Paul as precious in God's sight, we can see anyone as worthy of love.

When I see with faith and hope, I can choose not to focus on all the mistakes. If God walked into my house, He would embrace me and accept me just as I am. I might feel ashamed, unclean, or unworthy, but those emotions come because of my self-judgment and the belief that my identity is equal to my performance.

Paul experienced perfect love through Ananias *before* he did anything to earn it. In the same way, God loves people all the time regardless of their attitude or behavior. Our Advocate defends us and wants to transform our bitterness and accusations. We are holy and were chosen to be in His family—and all the people around us are accepted the same way. Our only reasonable response to such love should be gratitude and a willing heart to partner with God's abundant mercy for the world.

Praying for Your City

My teenage daughters, whom I love, sometimes make "interesting" decisions. Recently I had to confront one of them about a couple of situations, and I made what I believed to be a fair judgment concerning the consequences of her actions. In both situations, my daughter and I agreed on a payment plan for the damages that had occurred.

But when I presented the solution to God in prayer, I was surprised by His response. I felt like He told me to surrender my previous experiences and the wisdom I had gathered from reading several parenting books. I've learned a lot about raising children and usually lean on my experiences and all the reading I've done to help me discern the best course of action when dealing with my kids. But God wanted me to see the situation from a different perspective, and in order to receive that perspective, I needed to let go of the past.

He also told me to cut the consequences I'd arranged with my daughter in half. I was shocked and—let's just be honest here—completely frustrated that God would *interfere* with my leadership role. I didn't want to look weak in my daughter's eyes. When I told her what happened and that God had dramatically reduced the consequences for her, she brightened up and accepted this new judgment with joy.

Afterward I went back to God and listened carefully for His voice, because I wanted to understand what He was doing. I felt like He said He wanted me to partner with my daughter's restitution, which did not make sense to me at all.

"Mercy," He said.

My logical mind does not understand mercy and, unfortunately, my first thought usually is to resist mercy. When I hear about someone committing a crime, I want justice or payback. My daughter knows this about me, and we both jokingly agreed that this mercy *did not* come from me! I would never have come to this merciful judgment—unless God intervened.

As I opened my eyes to see how I could partner with what God was doing in my daughter's life, I stepped into agreement with good news. As her parent, too often I've been a source of *bad news* for her. The opposite of mercy.

We've been given an opportunity to partner with God's mercy and give it freely to everyone we meet. We need to stop worrying and being critical about the world and instead learn to listen to God's heart. Only then can we experience His peace that replaces our fears.

> Don't worry about anything; instead, pray about everything. Tell God what you need and thank him for all he has done. Then you will experience God's peace, which exceeds anything we can understand.
> Philippians 4:6-7

It is possible to learn to enjoy His judgments over our own. We need His perspective on *everything*, so we can maintain His peace toward everyone we encounter. The more I surrender to God's perspective about people, the more I feel my heart filling with light and freedom.

We are called to learn from our Father how to love everyone on earth. There is no argument that will ever conquer God's established mercy toward people. He will never allow us to reject or abandon anyone, no matter what they have done. "Are we not all children of the same Father? Are we not all created by the same God?" (Mal. 2:10).

Like it or not—and sometimes I find myself in the "not" category—we are invited to surrender every thought that would separate us from other people and become advocates for our cities. It is time to discover God's thoughts for the people He's put in our lives.

Intercession Point

> Look up the population of your city, and ask God to fill your heart with hope for each and every person. Pray for your city from a place of hope, and purpose to see everyone through the Lord's eyes of mercy.

Chapter 16
GOD'S BEAUTIFUL OBSESSION

A few years ago, I served meals at a local homeless outreach because I wanted to learn how to connect with people. One day during lunch, I walked around looking for someone to talk to. I approached two gentlemen who were eating together and started listening in on their conversation in hopes they would welcome me to join them.

They did not. They noticed my presence but continued their conversation without me.

One guy got up and returned with a plate of cantaloupe heavily dashed with black pepper. I'd never seen anyone put spicy pepper on a sweet melon before, so I asked if I could try a piece. The guy was more than willing to share, and I grabbed a piece off his plate with my fingers. To my surprise, I discovered it was really good.

After these two guys watched me eat off their plate with my dirty hands, the whole atmosphere changed. They immediately opened up to me and started asking me questions about my life. Within a short time, we became friends and they invited me to come and find them on the street so we could continue hanging out. Eating their food, just as they would eat it, made us equal.

Jesus said, "If you hear my voice and open the door, I will come in, and we will share a meal together as friends" (Rev. 3:20). Jesus is willing to eat our food, in our homes, and just be with us. When I ate with these guys, I communicated acceptance and value, without saying a word.

God once told me, "If you want to save a relationship, you first need to save your mind."

Our minds can build walls against the very thing the Holy Spirit is trying to do inside us. God *humbles* our minds so we can step into the destiny He's prepared. Our relationships will thrive when we forgive and truly start living out a lifestyle of grace toward one another.

When we're able to break down barriers and connect with people, we become good news and a picture of God's unconditional love toward them. Connection is more important than societal rules or performance. God reaches into a dirty world and embraces us as His own. He eats with dirty hands to reach the world He loves. His value for relationship over perfect behavior is good news. To embrace the world, we first need to surrender our comfort and our opinions about what we believe is acceptable behavior.

ADVOCATE

I don't know how many times I've gotten irritated at my kids because I had to remind them to wash their hands before eating. When one of them gets sick, the first thing I usually do is lecture her about proper handwashing and invisible germs. "Handwashing is an important routine and vital for a healthy society! This practice has saved many lives during surgeries or childbirth and prevents diseases from spreading!" All that's completely true. But when taken too far, routines that are intended to bring life can also cultivate a divisive culture that separates people.

During Jesus's day, certain conservative Jewish people were more religious about washing their hands than they were about seeking God (Mark 7:3-4). Jesus actually said their worship was a "farce" because they taught the rules of man as if they were the rules of God. "You ignore God's law and substitute your own tradition" (vv. 7-8). When good advice turns into "commands from God," we are using rules to empower ourselves and—as a natural result of a religious mindset—put others down. A legalistic mindset doesn't look to build others up but develops an attitude that devalues anyone who doesn't follow a similar lifestyle.

God is not looking for ways to separate His heart from people. However, it seems like a huge number of us *are*. We subtly search for ways we can separate ourselves from others by belittling them and tearing them down. Anytime we focus on how others don't measure up to the way we live, we're replacing God's law of love with our own beliefs. When we judge others, our so-called wisdom can blind us from seeing His heart for people. He doesn't want us to get distracted by trying to do His job—He wants us to focus on being generous, forgiving, and kind to one another.

Don't Be a Loggerhead

> How can you think of saying to your friend, "Let me help you get rid of that speck in your eye," when you can't see past the log in your own eye?
>
> Matthew 7:4

We're the ones who put the "log" in our eyes, so we also have the ability to pull it out—to clear up our distorted perspective. We can choose to listen to God's quiet voice more than other people's opinions. We can cling to His love for us and for other people instead of the "rules" we think allow us to put down those who don't conform to them. This kind of negative perspective needs to be removed from our vision so we can see ourselves and other people clearly.

God designed us to see ourselves through eyes of compassion, not criticism. What would that be like? Our self-evaluation can become a blinding log in our eyes and distract us from simply being loved by God and fully present with other people. That's the goal—simple love.

Jesus made it very clear that we have the ability to recover our vision:

> First get rid of the log in your own eye; then you will see well enough to deal with the speck in your friend's eye.
>
> Matthew 7:5

ADVOCATE

The word *hypocrite* in Greek is *hupokrités,* which means an actor, pretender, or one who answers. When broken down, the word comes from two ideas: The first part means "judging," and the other part means "under," like someone who is hiding behind a mask.[1] In other words, a hypocrite is someone who answers on God's behalf and pretends to see—when they're actually just a blind imposter. They act like they're a master of certain virtues when they don't practice those virtues consistently.

But when we get rid of the log in our eyes, we will see. The word *see* in Greek is *diablepó* and means to look through something and see clearly.[2]

So first, we need to see ourselves accurately and understand we are truly loved and valued by God. When our hearts are free from judgment and surrendered to the Lord, we can see other people clearly and help them. This kind of vision can *look through* the masks others wear to see their hidden wounds with empathy. Genuine spiritual sight steps into the realm of prophecy and hearing the Holy Spirit's voice. God can give us prophetic insights, but without love and humility, those insights can't move forward and do what He intends.

People are allergic to imposters who try to act their way through life, but we become beacons of hope when we choose to develop a humble and compassionate attitude. Vulnerability opens the door to truly help people who are struggling.

---

1 Strong's Greek #5273.
2 Strong's Greek #1227.

Second, we can help *only* those we value as friends. A friend will let you stick your fingers in their eye, but a stranger won't let you close enough to help them. Friends are vulnerable with each other and trust that when they expose their weaknesses, they won't be slammed with a shaming lecture.

Jesus didn't talk about helping people He didn't care about. People were attracted to Him because His love was real and genuine. If we want to bless others, we need to surrender all our divisive judgments so we can simply be their friends. God wants to teach us how to be open books that allow people to see who we are, even the places where we've failed. A safe atmosphere can turn strangers into trusted friends, and when our vision is clear of judgments, everyone can potentially become a friend.

What does *being a friend* look like in real life?

Jesus demonstrated His judgment-free mindset when He connected with prostitutes, drunkards, and those rejected as the worst in society. His eyes were free of prejudice. Even when He saw unhealthy issues, He focused on pointing out the positives and encouraging people to move forward.

A religious man named Simon once invited Jesus to dinner. Sometime that evening, a notoriously immoral woman interrupted their meeting. Jesus didn't tell her to come back at a more suitable time, when no one was there to mock her. Instead he told Simon:

ADVOCATE

> Look at this woman kneeling here. When I entered your home, you didn't offer me water to wash the dust from my feet, but she has washed them with her tears and wiped them with her hair. You didn't greet me with a kiss, but from the time I first came in, she has not stopped kissing my feet. You neglected the courtesy of olive oil to anoint my head, but she has anointed my feet with rare perfume.
>
> I tell you, her sins—and they are many—have been forgiven.
>
> Luke 7:44-47

To be honest, I relate more to Simon in this story than the thankful lady! When I've visited rough neighborhoods or city jails, the first thing that comes to my mind is how destructive people's actions can be—not just to them but to society in general. I think about the countless lives that have been ruined by senseless violence, greedy drug dealers, and human trafficking. Sometimes I become frustrated as I walk through rich financial districts and my mind starts to dwell on corruption, crooked politicians, and war profiteers.

My eyes need to be cleared of these judgments, so I can do what Jesus told Simon to do: *"Look at this woman."*

When I look at the world to see its weaknesses, a huge log of accusation starts to blind me. The list of wrongs goes on and on, and it blocks out all the good. When I focus on someone else's shortcomings, I deflect attention from my own failure-to-perform and build up my sense of self-righteousness.

Simon and I could be buddies. He and his friends were so distracted by the judgmental culture they lived in that he didn't even offer Jesus the common courtesies of the day (vv. 44, 46). He preferred to find fault instead.

> When the Pharisee who had invited him saw this, he said to himself, "If this man were a prophet, he would know what kind of woman is touching him. She's a sinner!"
> Luke 7:39

Simon's mindset was full of self-righteousness—he actually thought he knew more than God Himself. This way of thinking prevents us from valuing others and treating them with respect. When we think we have all the answers, we become "blind guides leading the blind" (Matt. 15:14). We might use different words and facial expressions, but we all struggle with judging people and not seeing their true value.

If love is the goal, then the woman in this story outshone Simon and all his friends. The ones who seem to *fail* the test just might be capable of teaching everyone else.

God is obsessed with mercy, and He wants to highlight those who have received His mercy and are now freely giving it away. This woman had nothing left. Her pride and reputation were shattered, and she had nothing but mercy to lean on. If we're going to learn to love from a grateful heart, we need to stop trusting in our status or social ranking. Simon was too busy defending his reputation to see love in action. But Jesus wasn't worried about His reputation and therefore could see the gold within this broken woman.

In order to look past the world's many sins, we first need to understand that our sins—which are many—have been forgiven. We need to resist living in a performance mindset that is fixated on judging the world. Our simple goal should be to love our neighbors as ourselves—something we cannot do if we're holding grudges against everyone (Lev. 19:18).

God constantly defends us against accusations (Rev. 12:10), so how about we stand with Him and defend our neighbors? He wants us to partner with His love by giving Him all our thoughts of judgment and listening instead to His heart of mercy.

Extraordinary Consequence

Recently while I was praying, I saw an old man's face in my mind's eye. His skin was aged and weathered, but his eyes were bright and glistened with hope. I heard God say, "Nobody is old whose eyes are open."

Regardless of how insignificant or trivial our daily lives may feel, how we see the world has extraordinary consequences. I don't want anger and bitterness to rob me of entering God's joy for the world—I want to stay young in spirit and filled with hope for everyone I see.

One morning I felt troubled over a friend's lifestyle choices that were causing this person pain and anguish. I stopped myself and decided to ask God what *He* thought about this person and their situation.

I felt Him reply, "This person is a blessing." That was all I heard.

I had to hand over all my "wise" insights about this person's life in order to see what God saw—that they were a blessing and a gift to the world.

When we see the people around us as blessings, our perspective is finally correct and in line with God's heart for the world. Kindness doesn't need to decide if someone's lifestyle is positive or negative. We aren't called to defend people with our own reasoning, and we can't use logic to argue who is worth loving.

Praying for Your City

Recently I visited a city surrounded by farms. Every morning I could smell the fertilizer in the air, and my car would have a fine coating of manure-laced dust upon it.

As I interceded for this city, I saw a picture in my spirit that encouraged me to keep blessing every city I visited. In this picture, I saw a neighborhood of suburban homes. A person walked out their front door, picked up their garden hose, turned it on, and dropped it to the ground, allowing the water to flood their front yard and pour into the street. Then the next-door neighbor came out their front door and did the same thing. This repeated down the street until every house had its garden hose on full blast, flooding the yard. The water grew so deep that it formed a river, which overflowed into the city and continued out beyond the city, saturating the surrounding farmland.

At first I thought, *What a careless waste of water.* But slowly I began to realize this was what the land needed in order to produce a harvest.

Words of blessing cause *life* to spring up everywhere. I believe God wants to start a movement of people who stand up to bless their cities instead of curse them. It begins as each individual blesses their own household, then their neighbors' houses, then their city, then their nation—speaking excessive blessing, more than what seems necessary. Blessing that flows freely and is not restricted by criticism or judgment. It's time for us to hold our tongues when we feel like lashing out or speaking curses and, instead, throw open the wells of blessing.

Every prayer we speak concerning our cities needs to be led by our God of love. Intercession, at its core, is a choice to listen to His heart and mind instead of our own. It means stepping into an endless outpouring of His mercy and surrendering every accusation to happily become an advocate for the world.

Intercession Point

Ask God to show you how you can speak blessing over your city on a daily basis. This might be something unique! Bless the people who cut you off in traffic, who are rude and don't seem to care about you, who vote differently than you do, or who live extreme lifestyles. Try to see them the way God does, and pray they would encounter His hope and mercy.

ADVOCATE

For more information on loving your city,
visit www.brianheltsley.com

Bibliography

Pytches, Mary. *A Healing Fellowship: Guide to Practical Counselling in the Local Church*. London: Hodder & Stoughton Religious, 1988.

Strong, James. *The New Strong's Exhaustive Concordance of the Bible*. Expanded edition. Nashville: Thomas Nelson, 2010.

www.ingramcontent.com/pod-product-compliance
Lightning Source LLC
Chambersburg PA
CBHW061322040426
42444CB00011B/2736